I0480122

Mike's Mind Bending Mandelas Coloring Book

Mike F. Capshaw

Copyright © 2019 Mike Capshaw

All rights reserved.

ISBN: 9781798976043

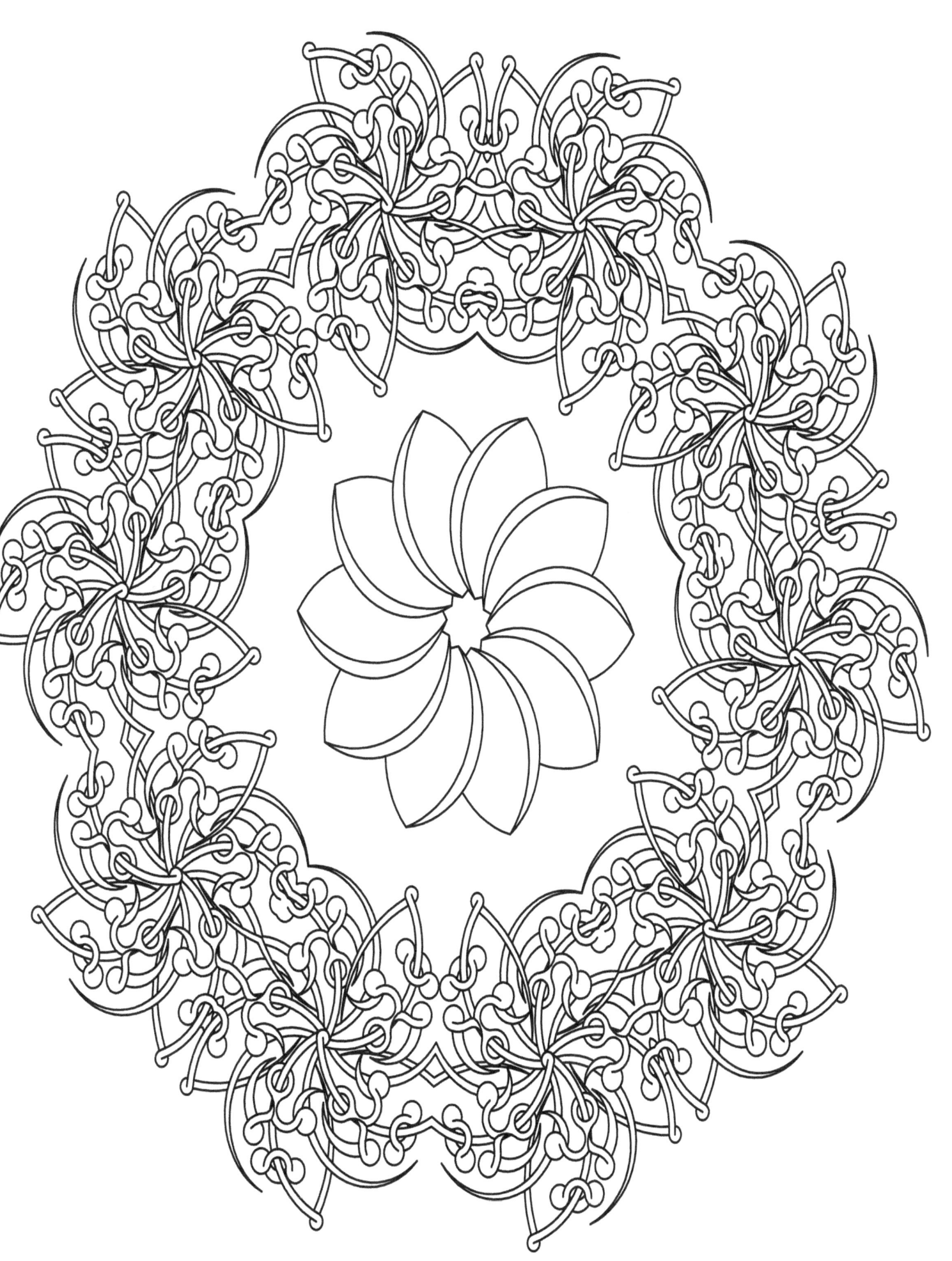

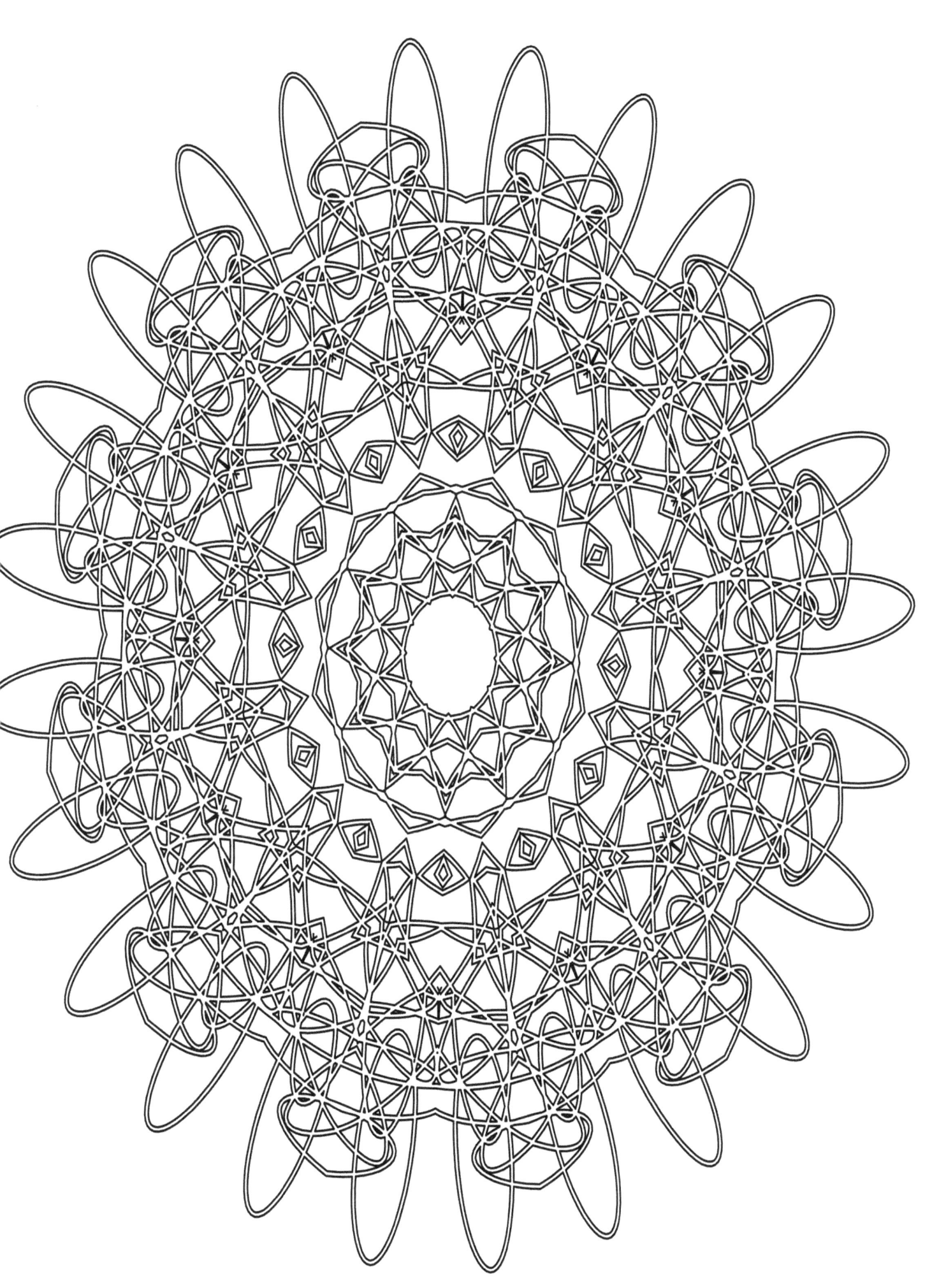

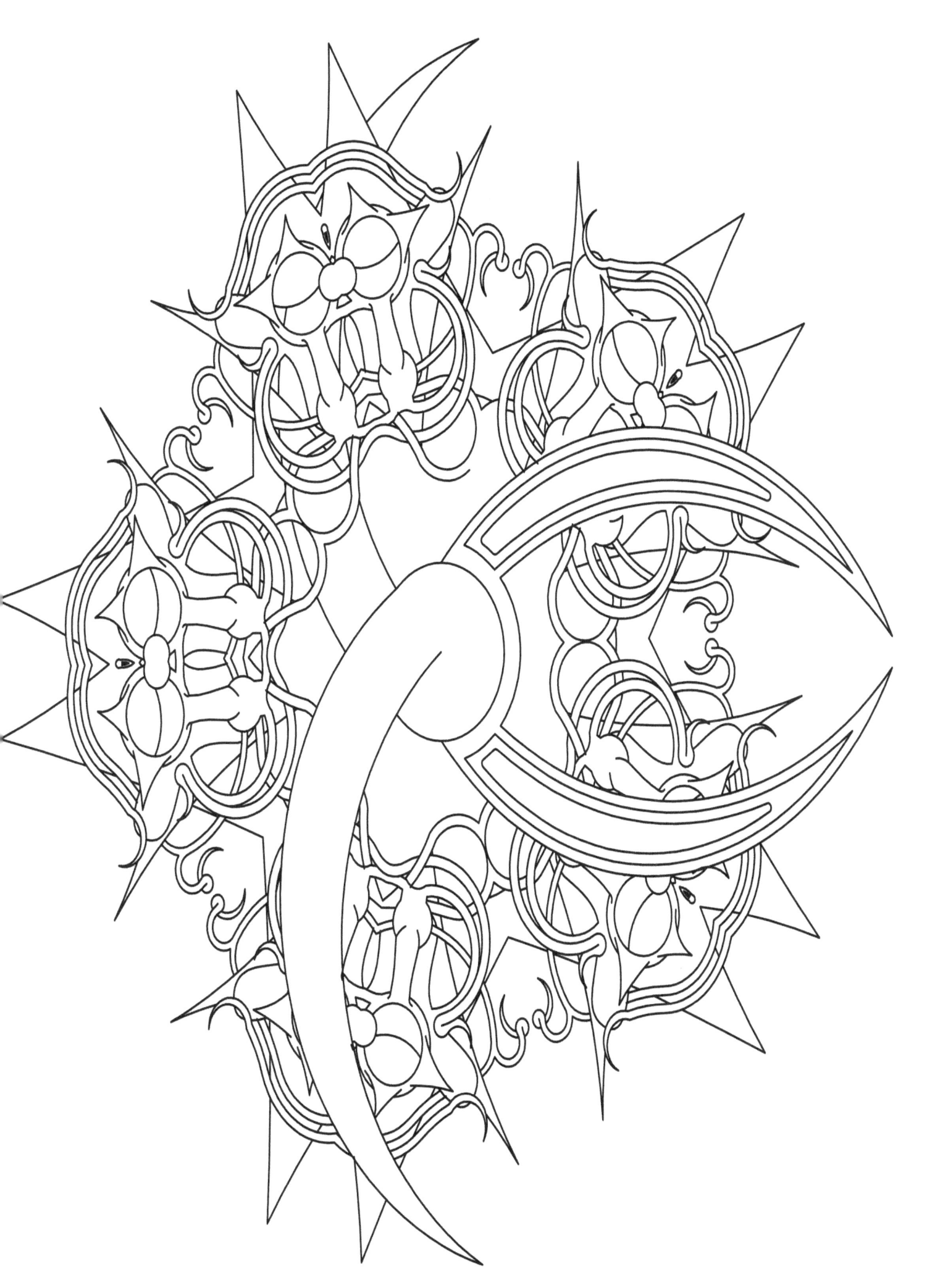

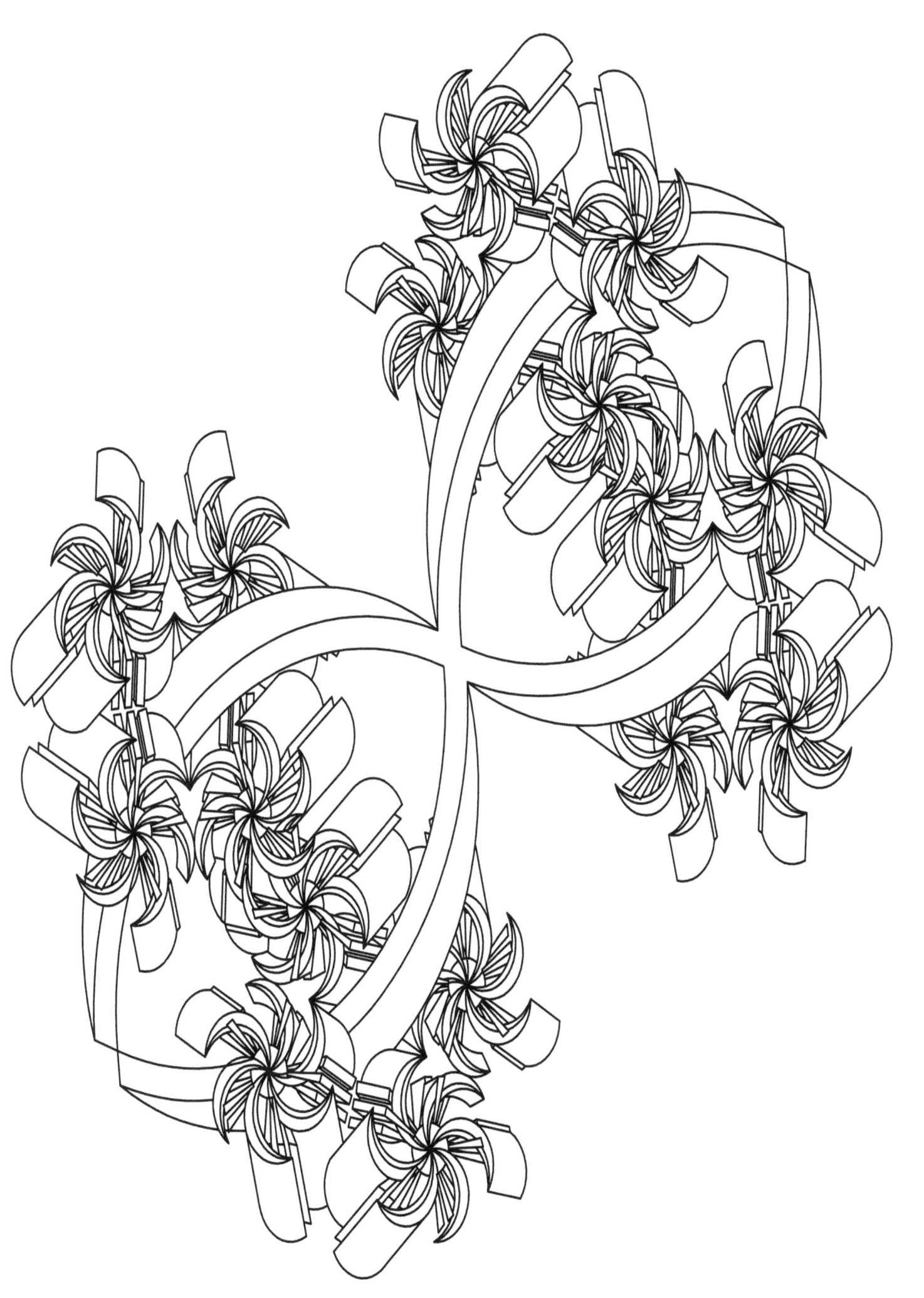

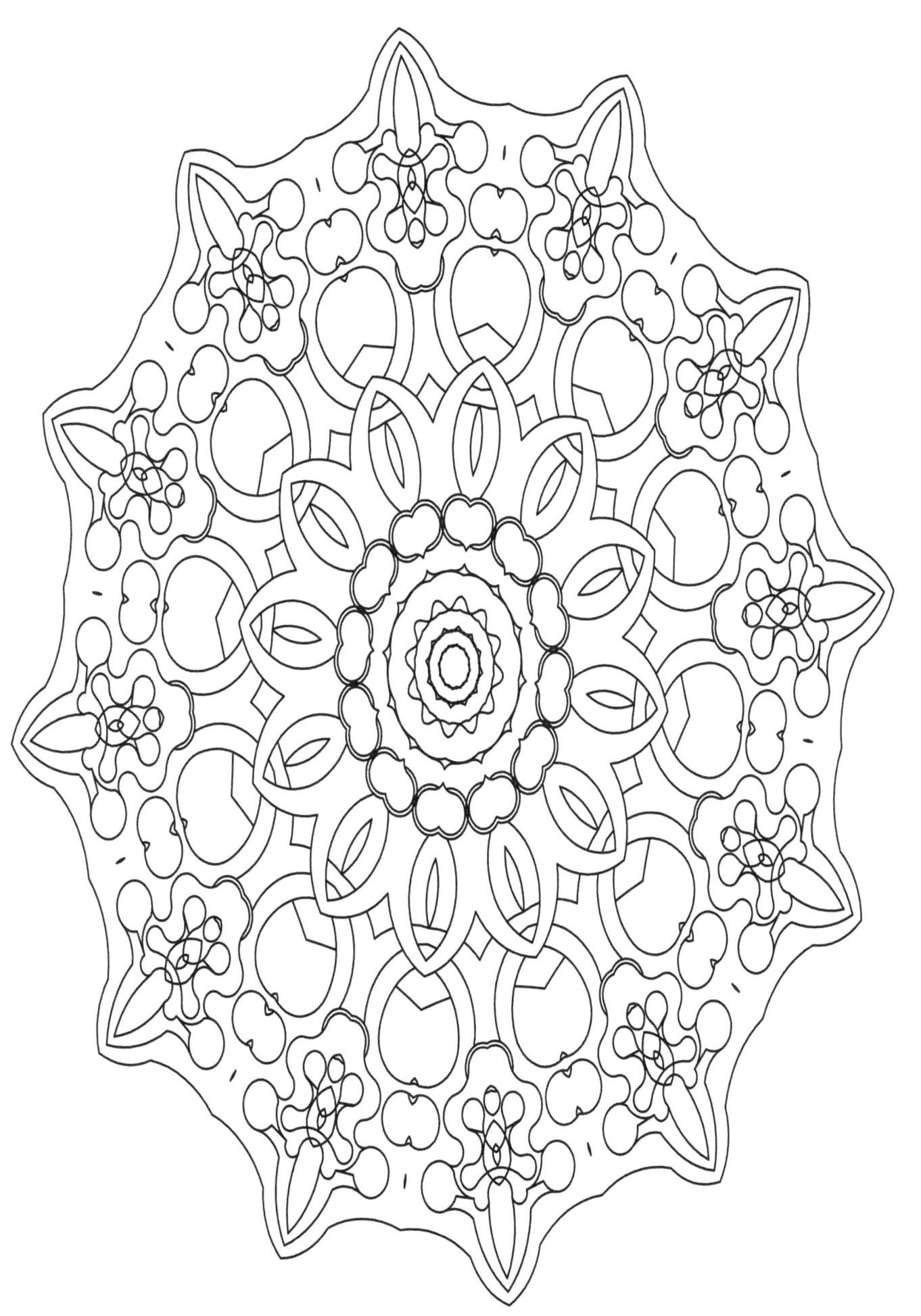

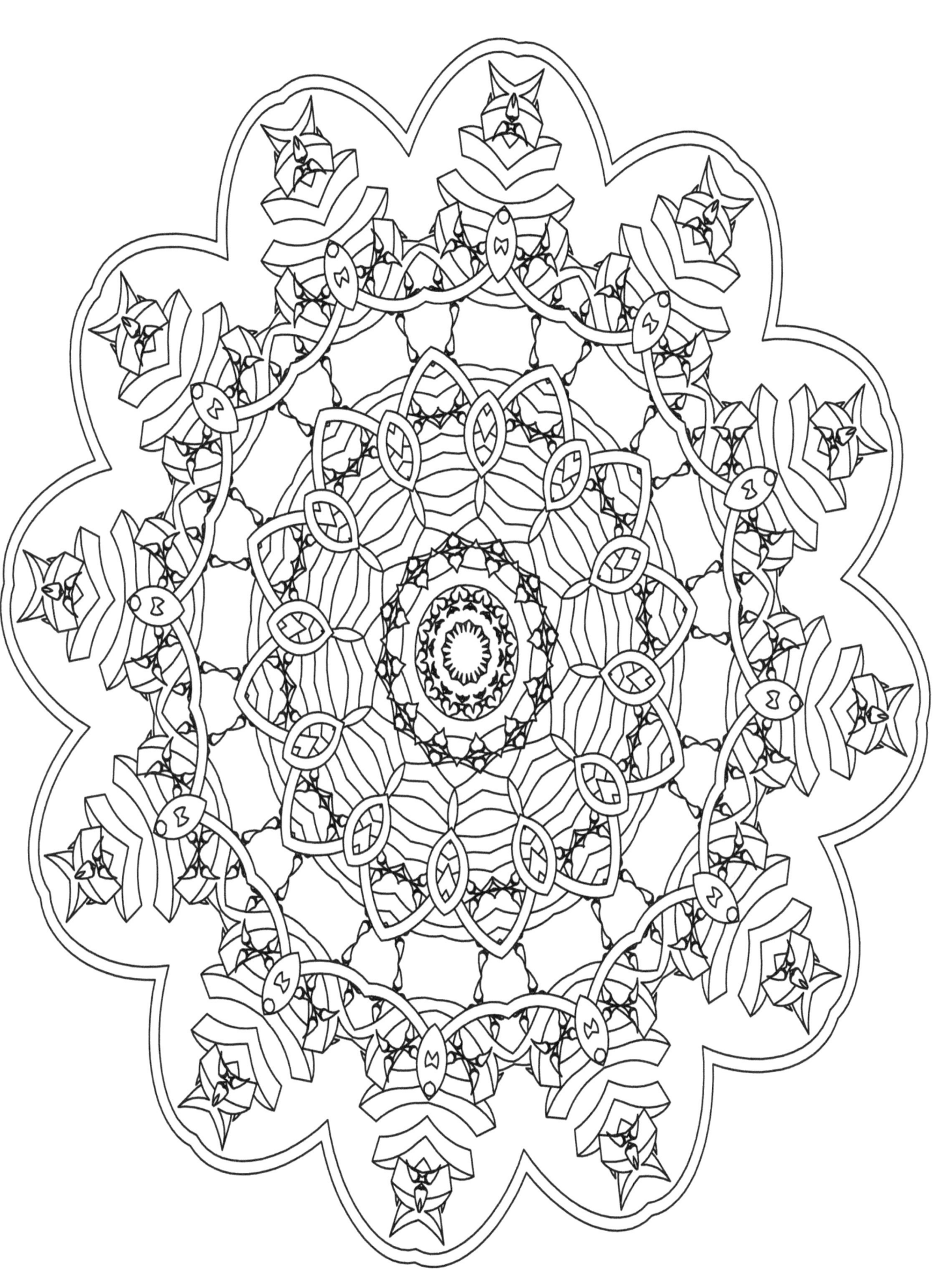

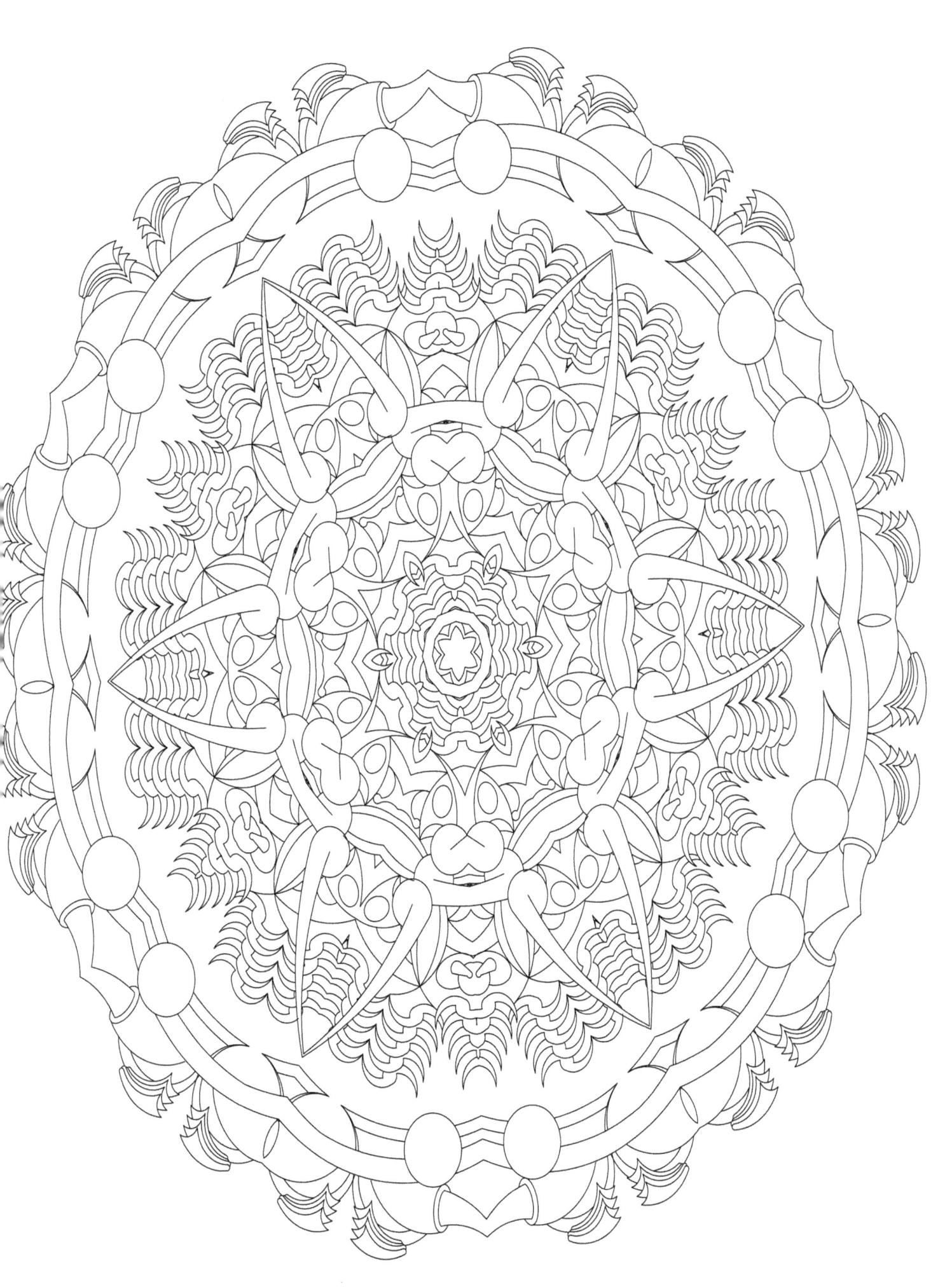

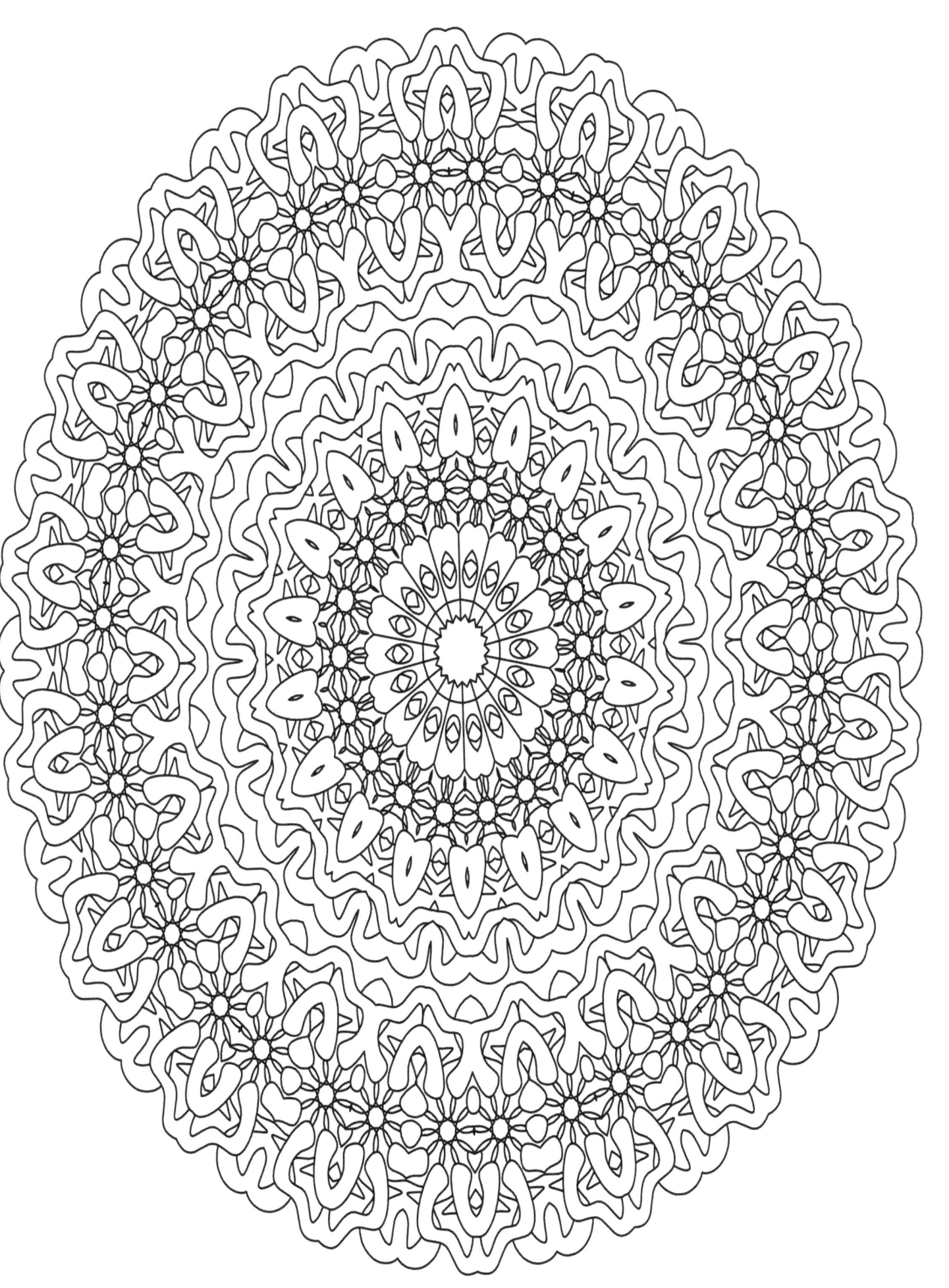

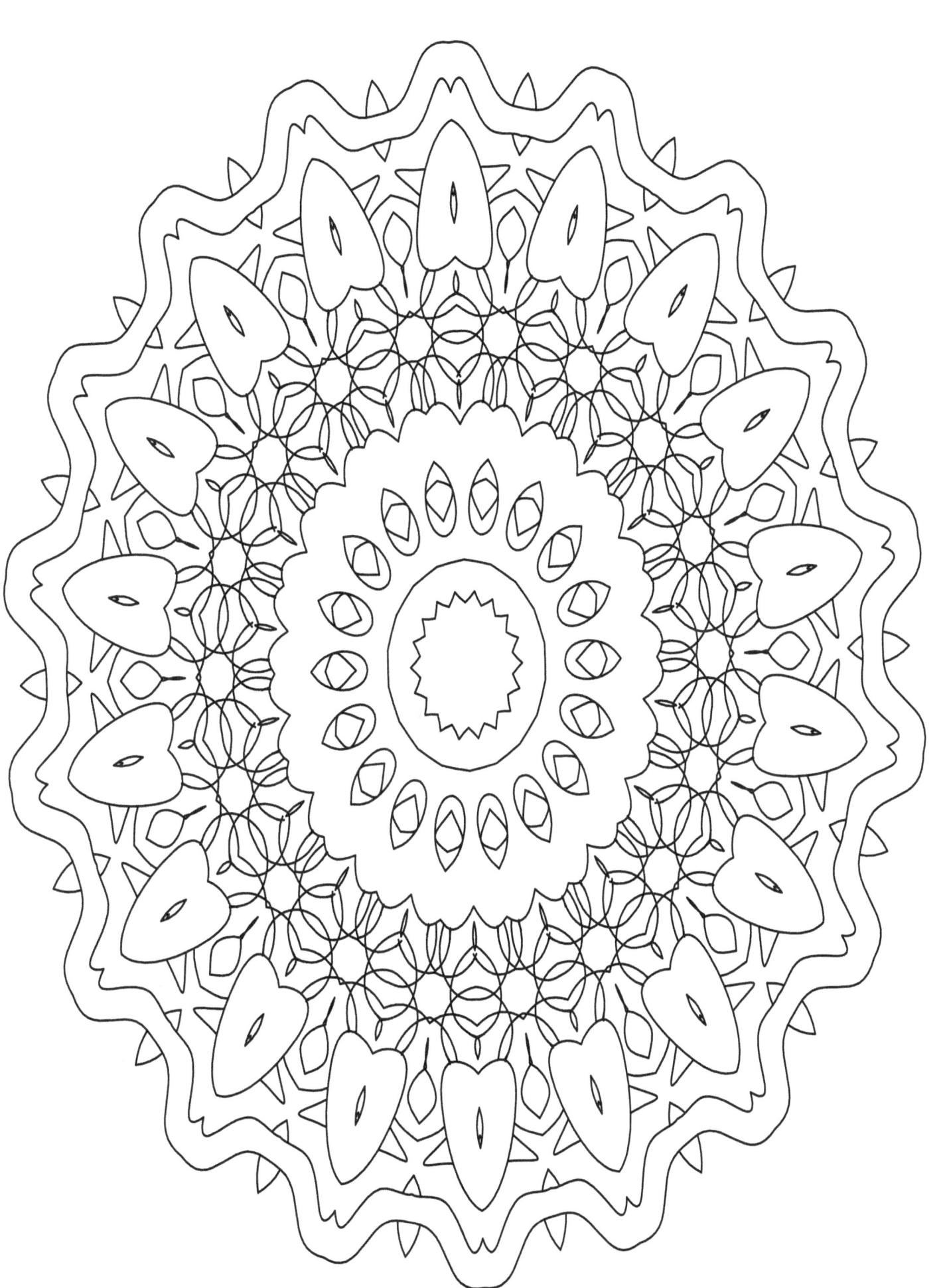

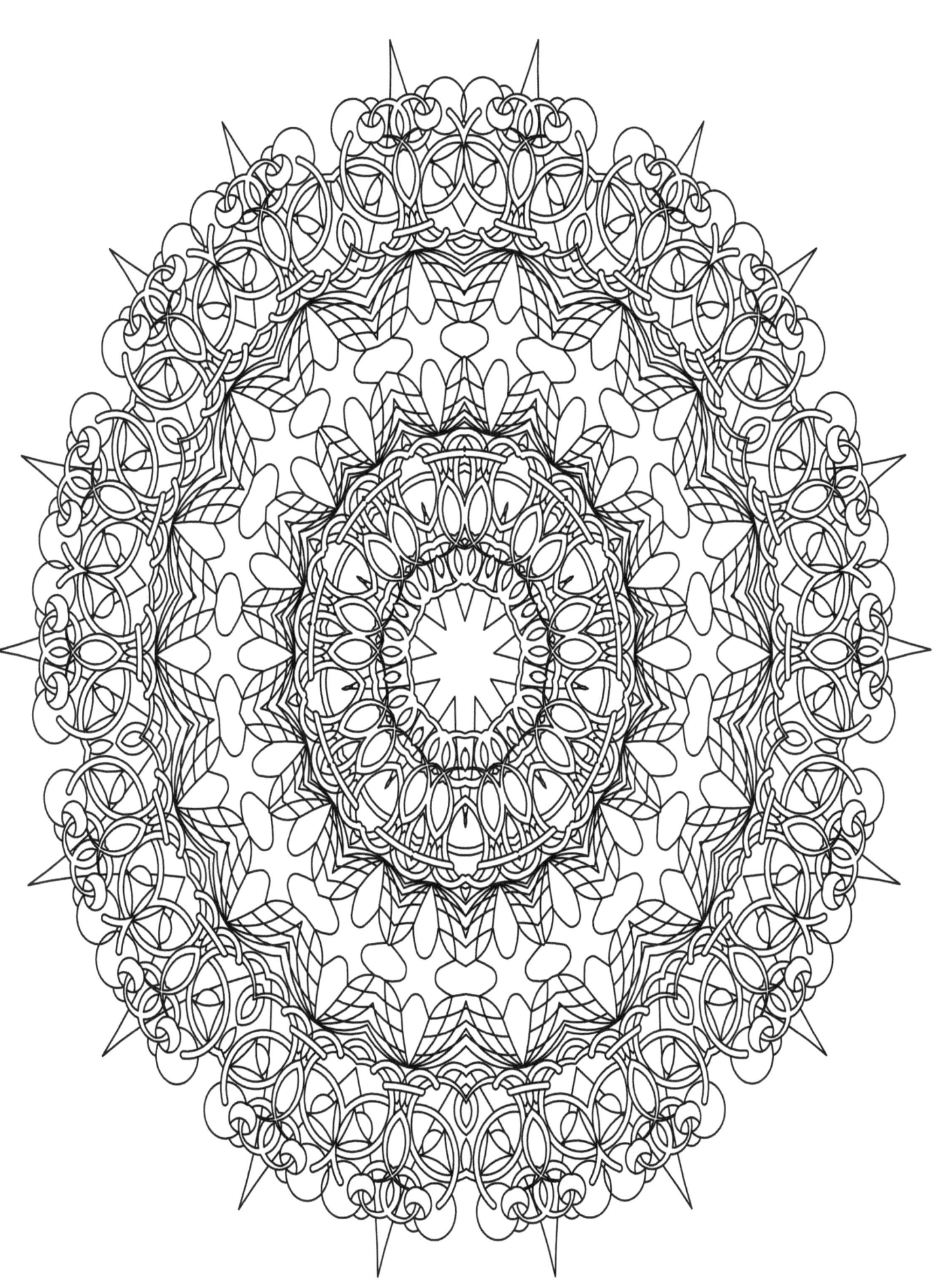

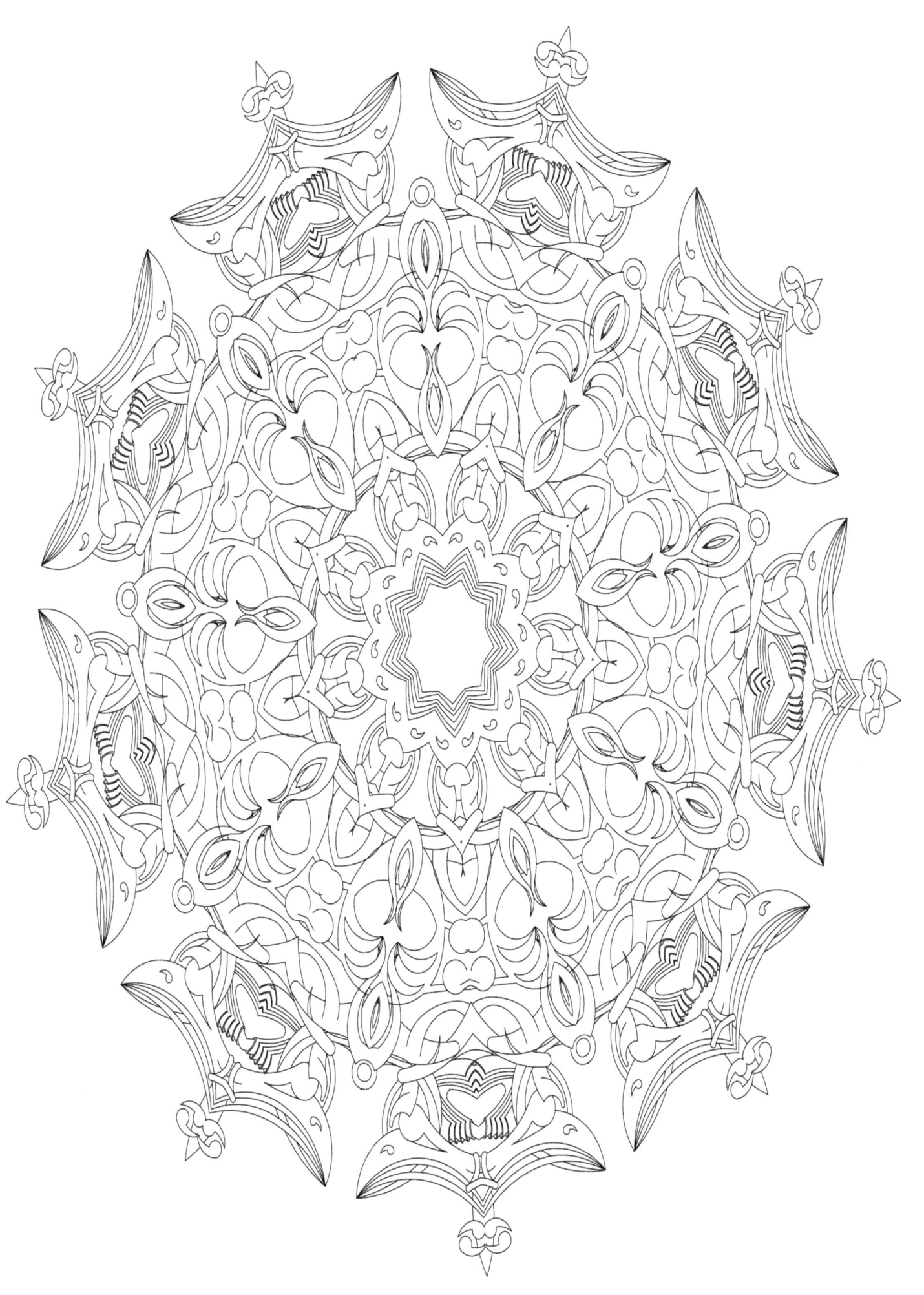

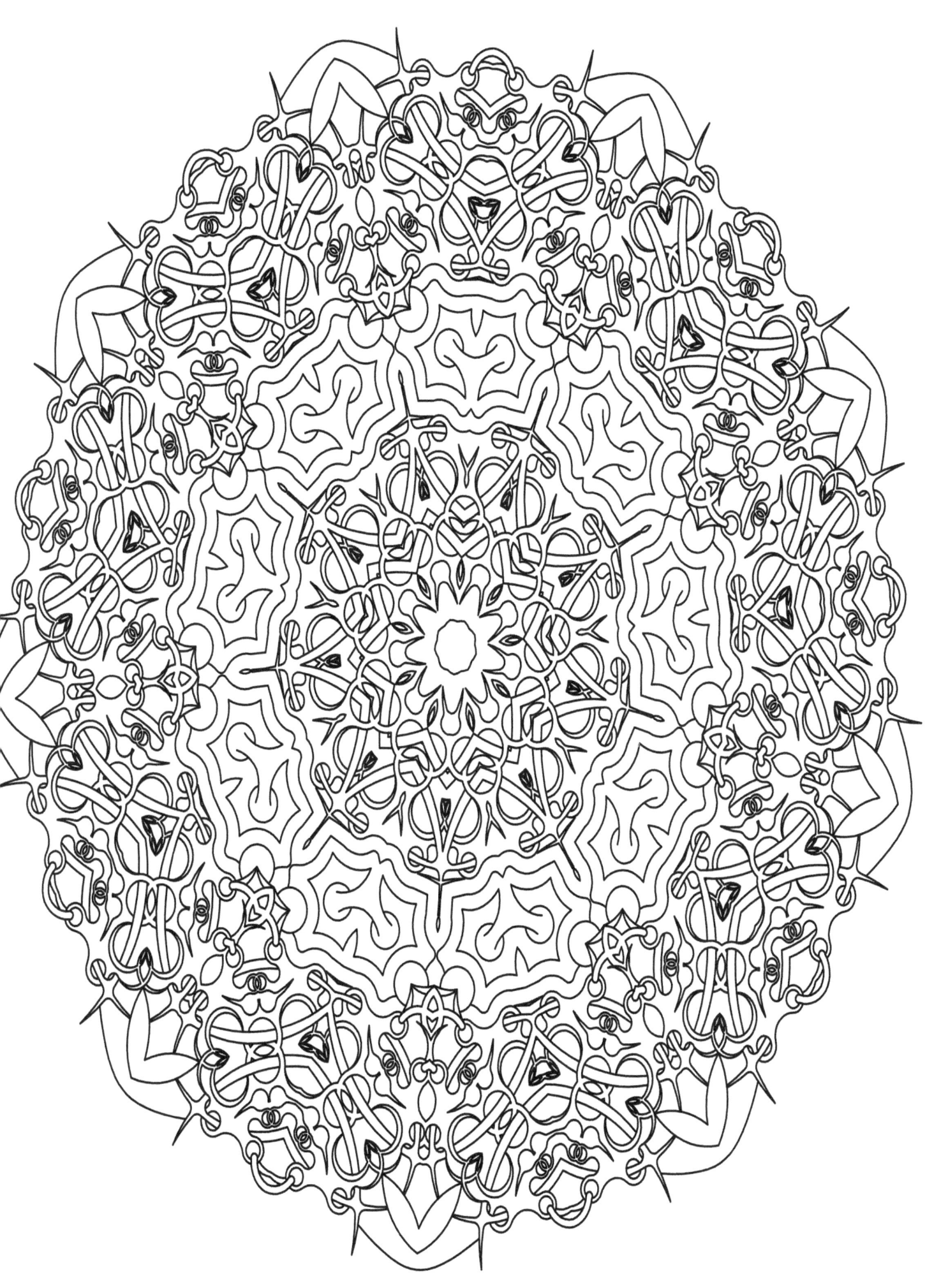

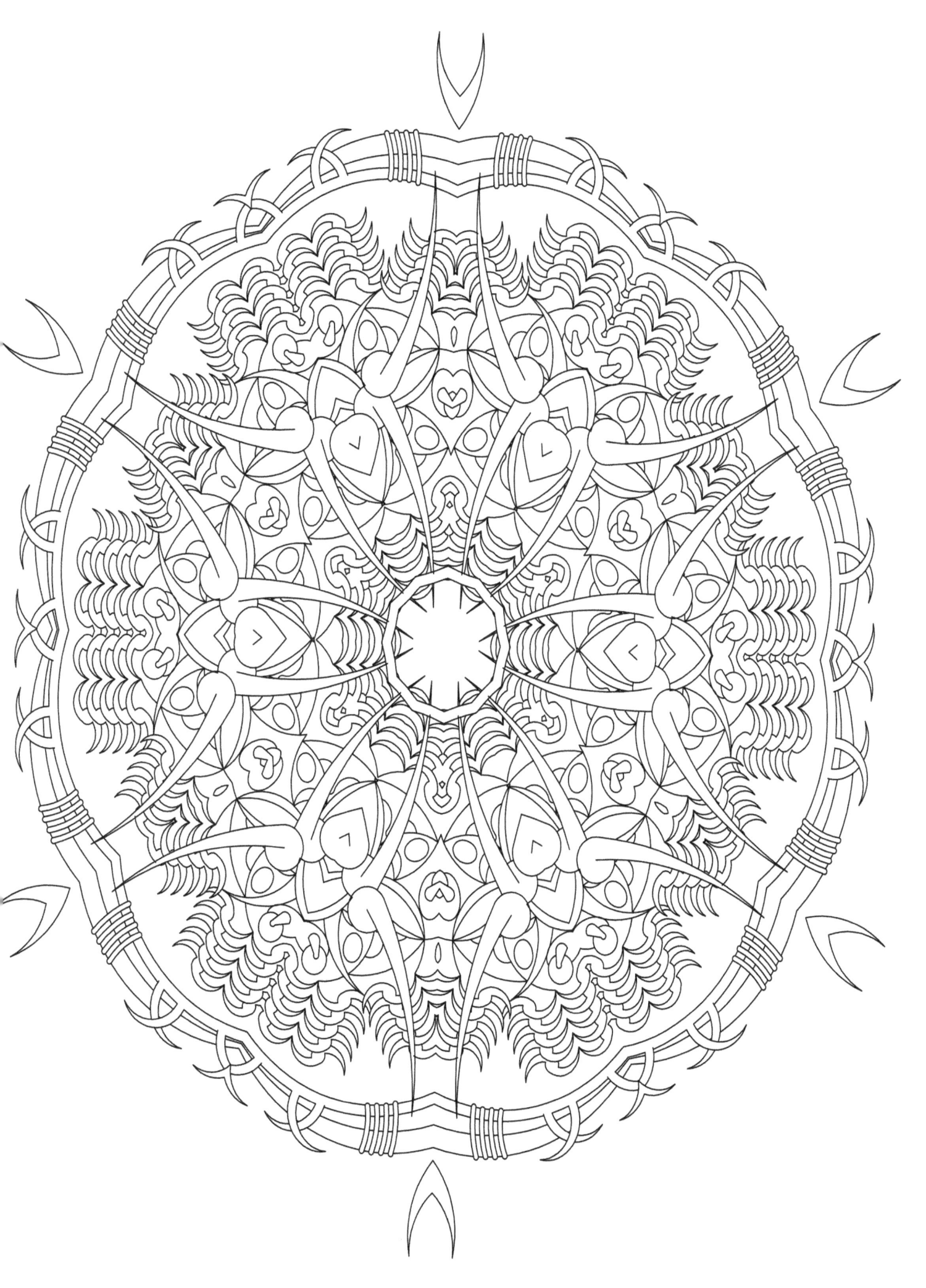

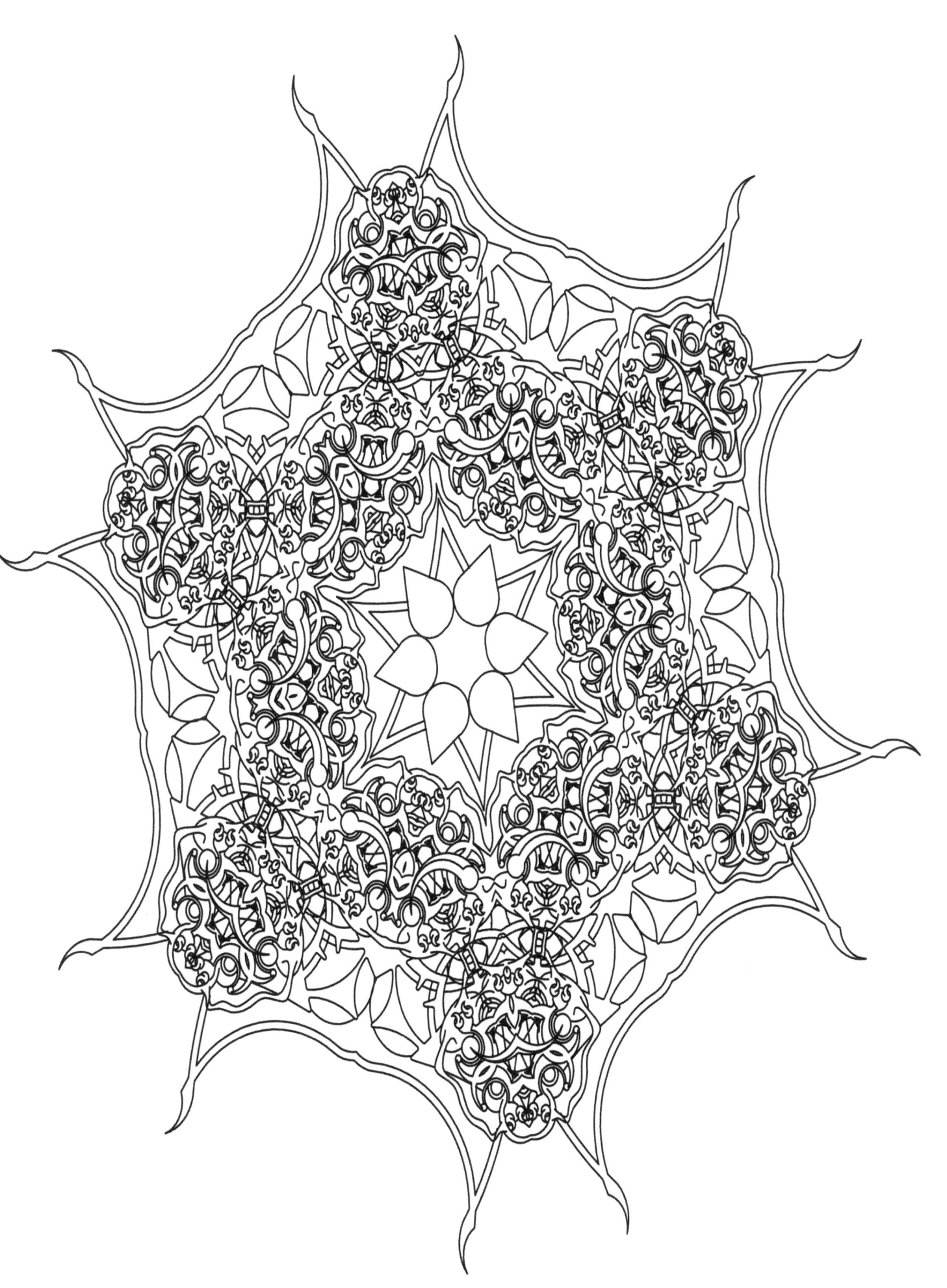

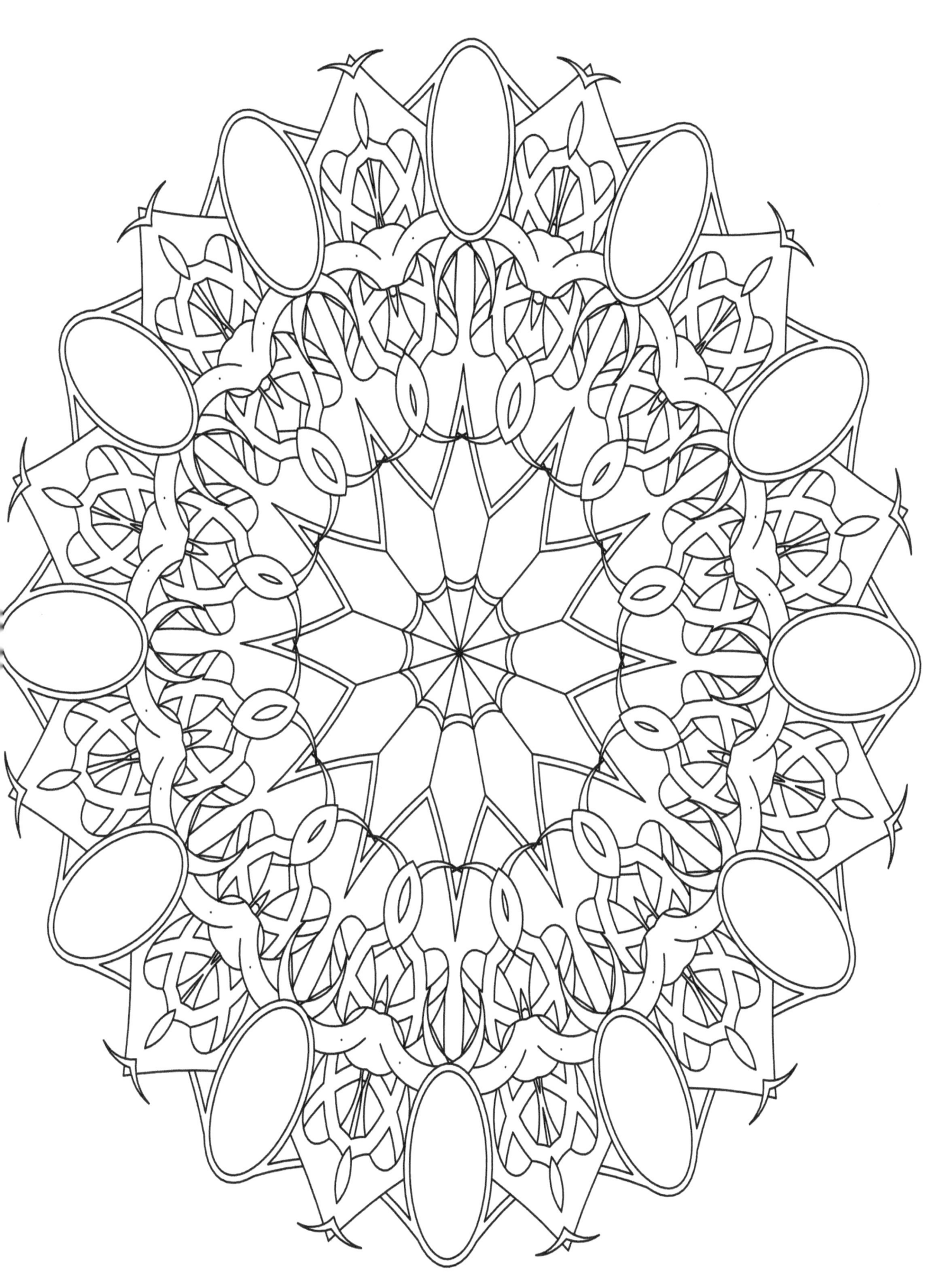

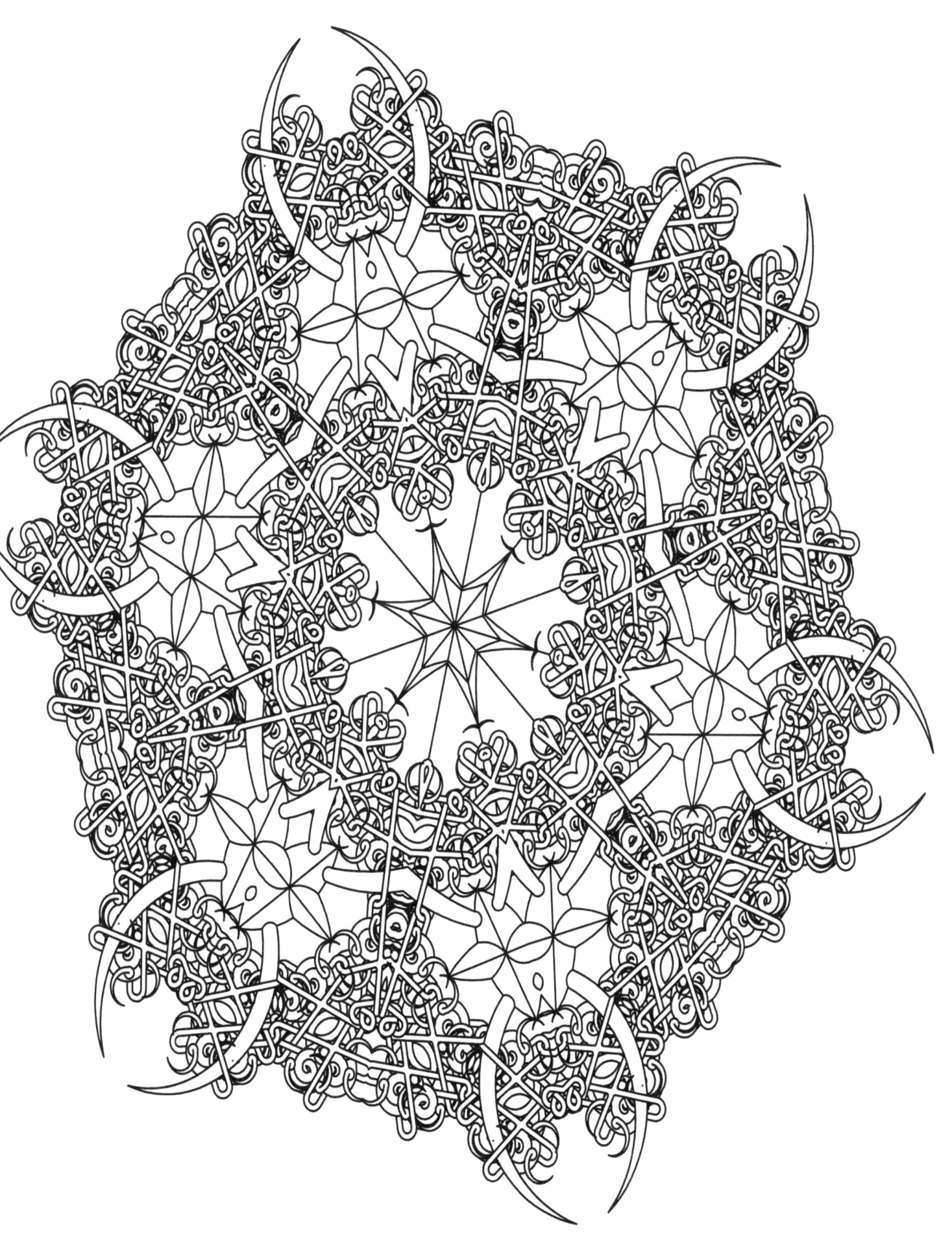

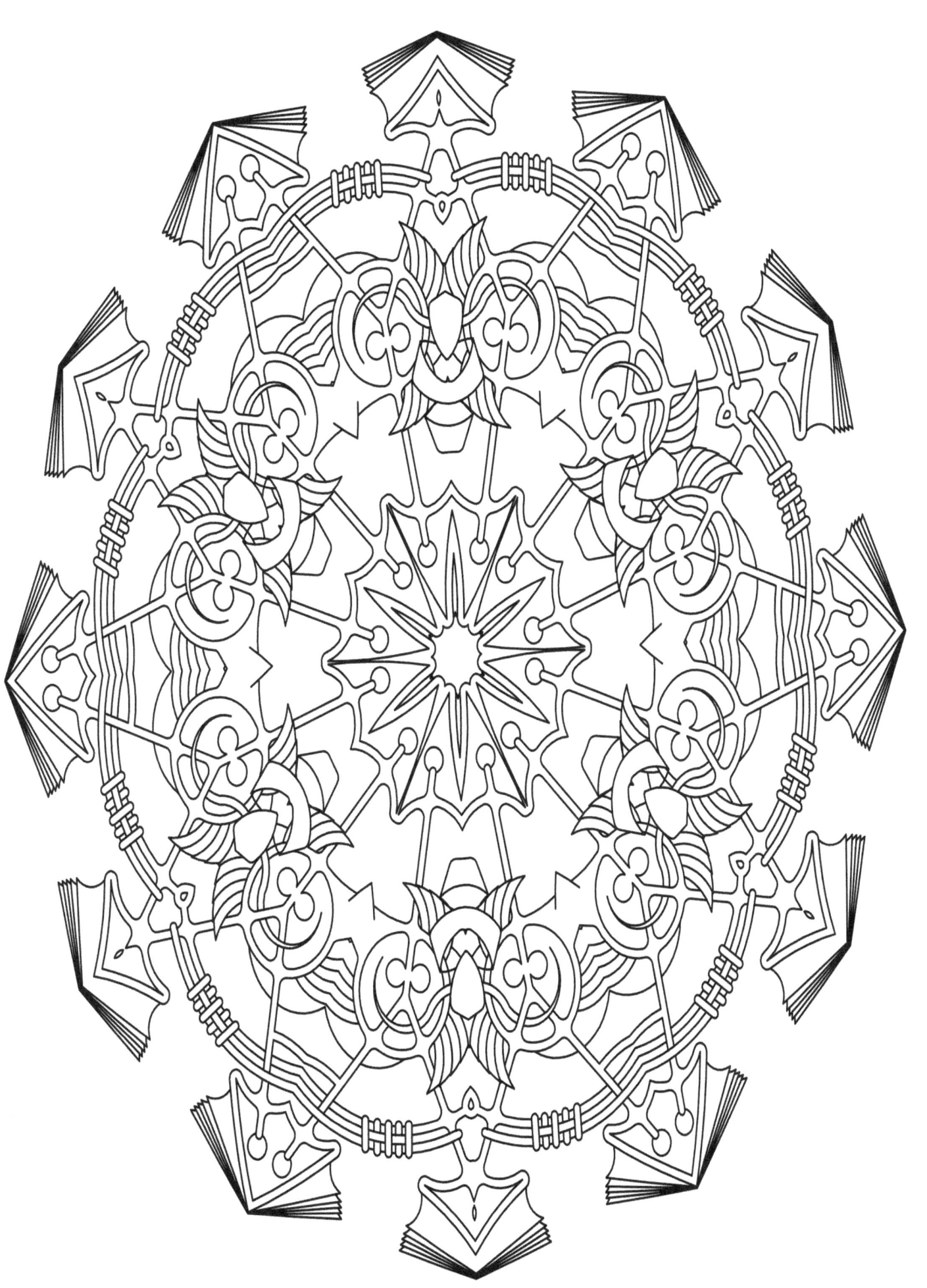

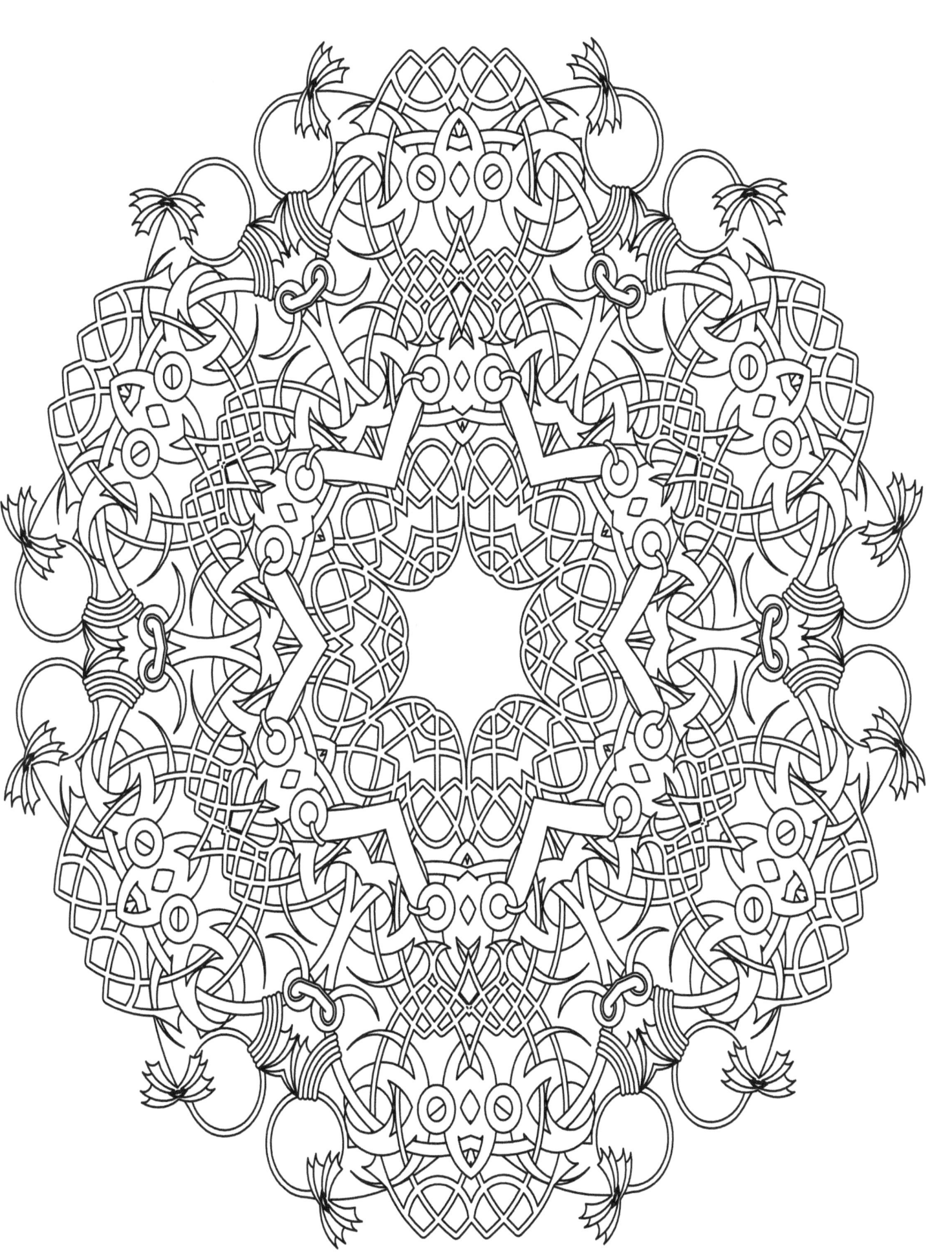

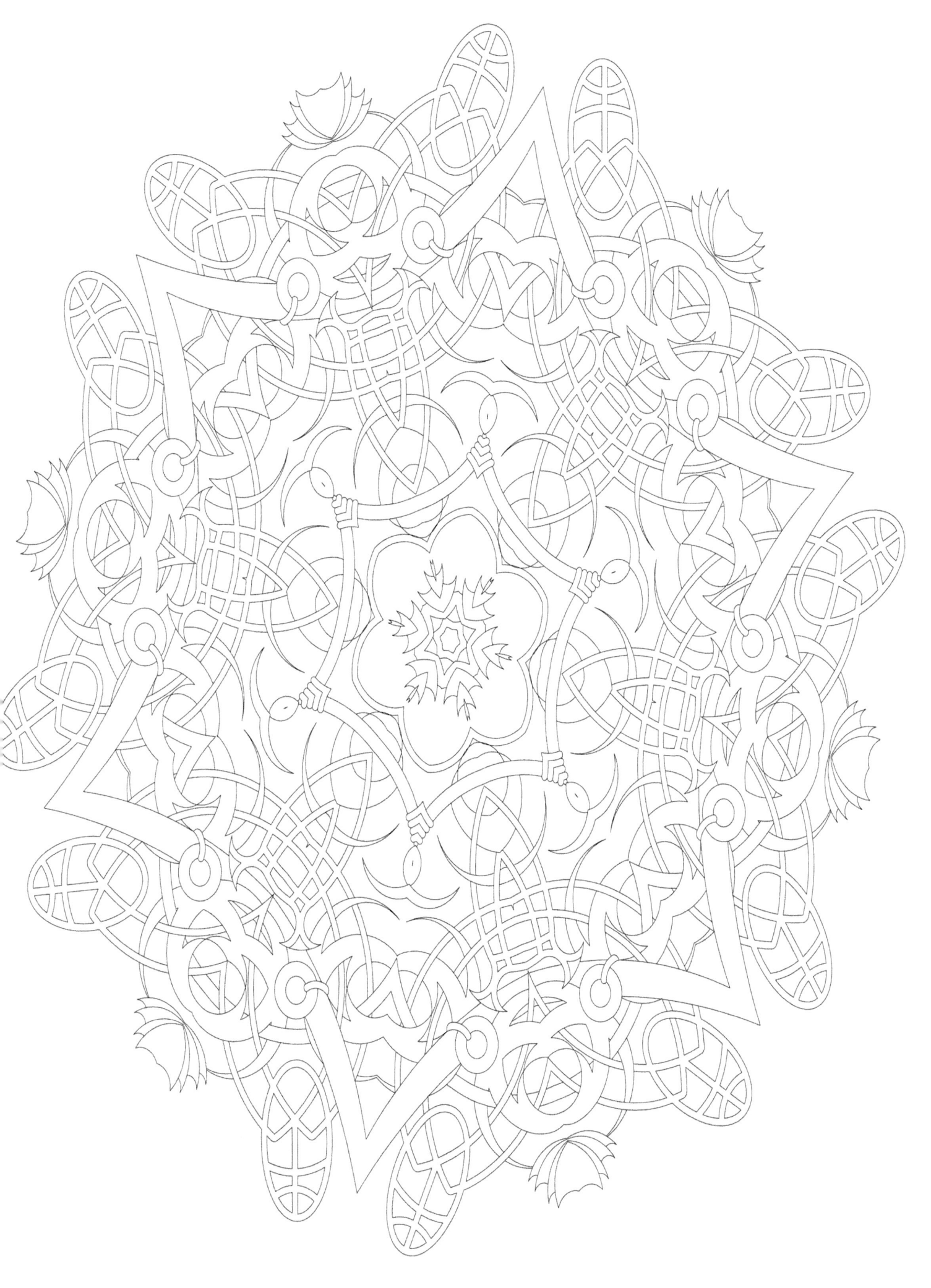

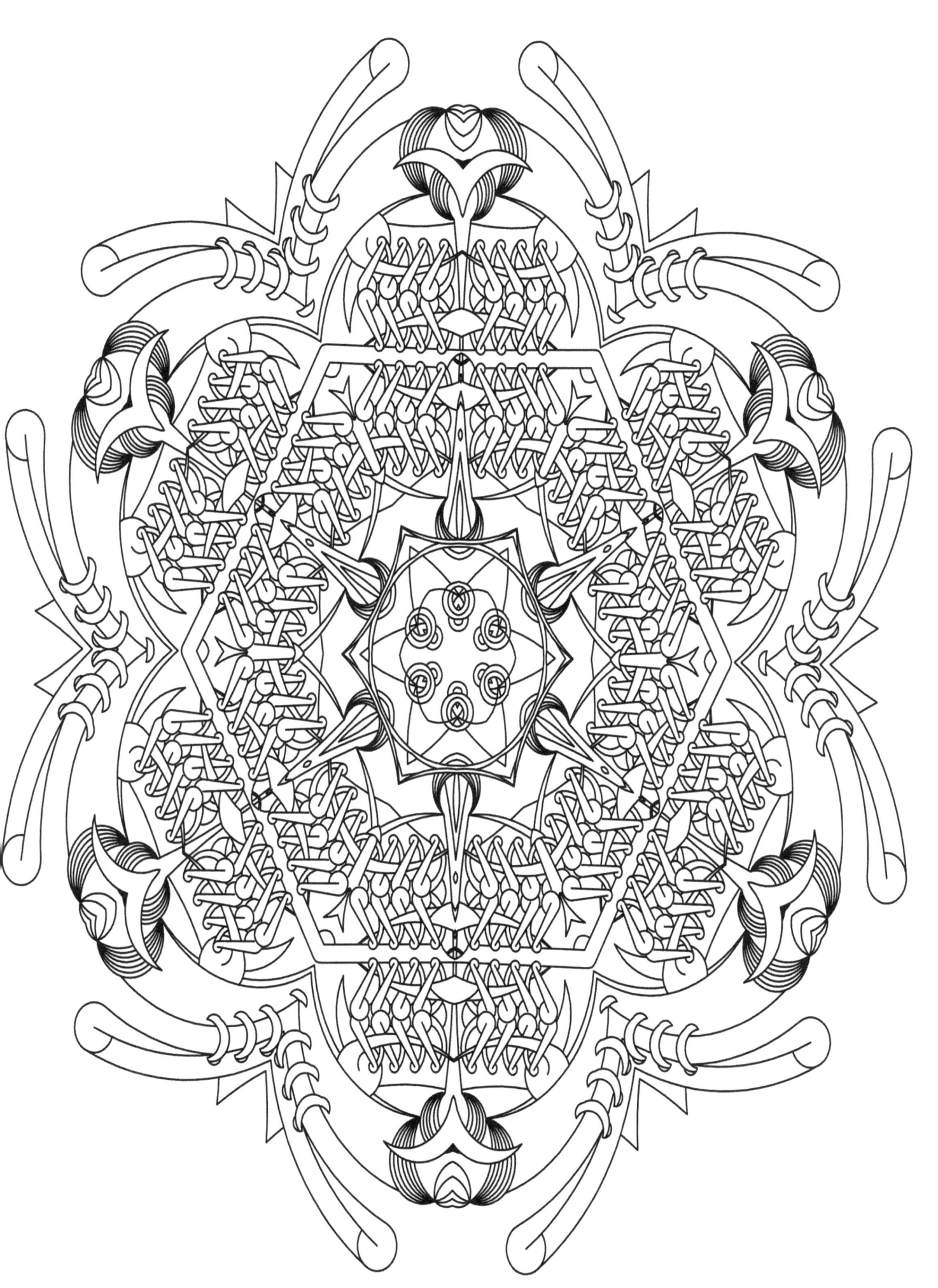

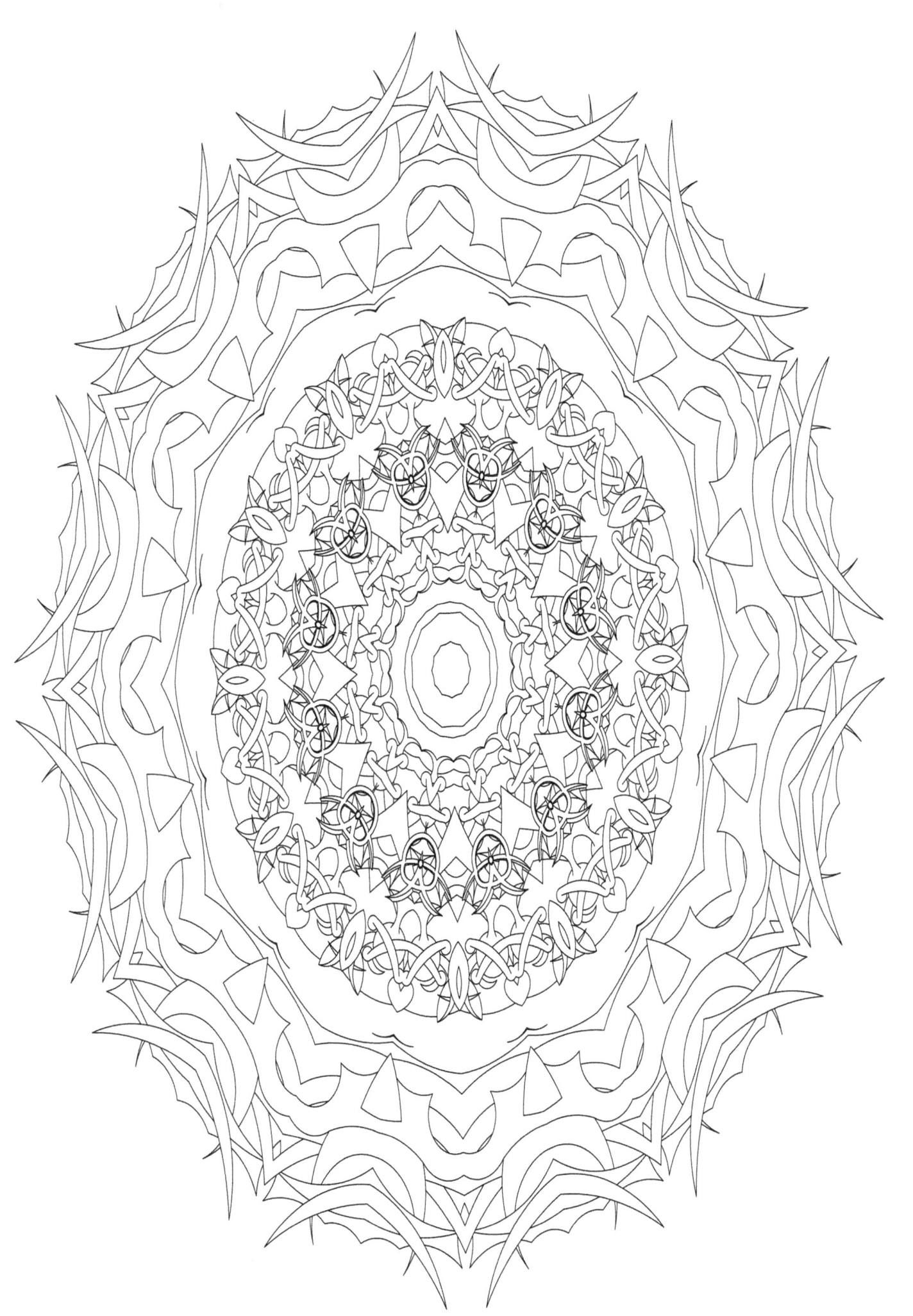

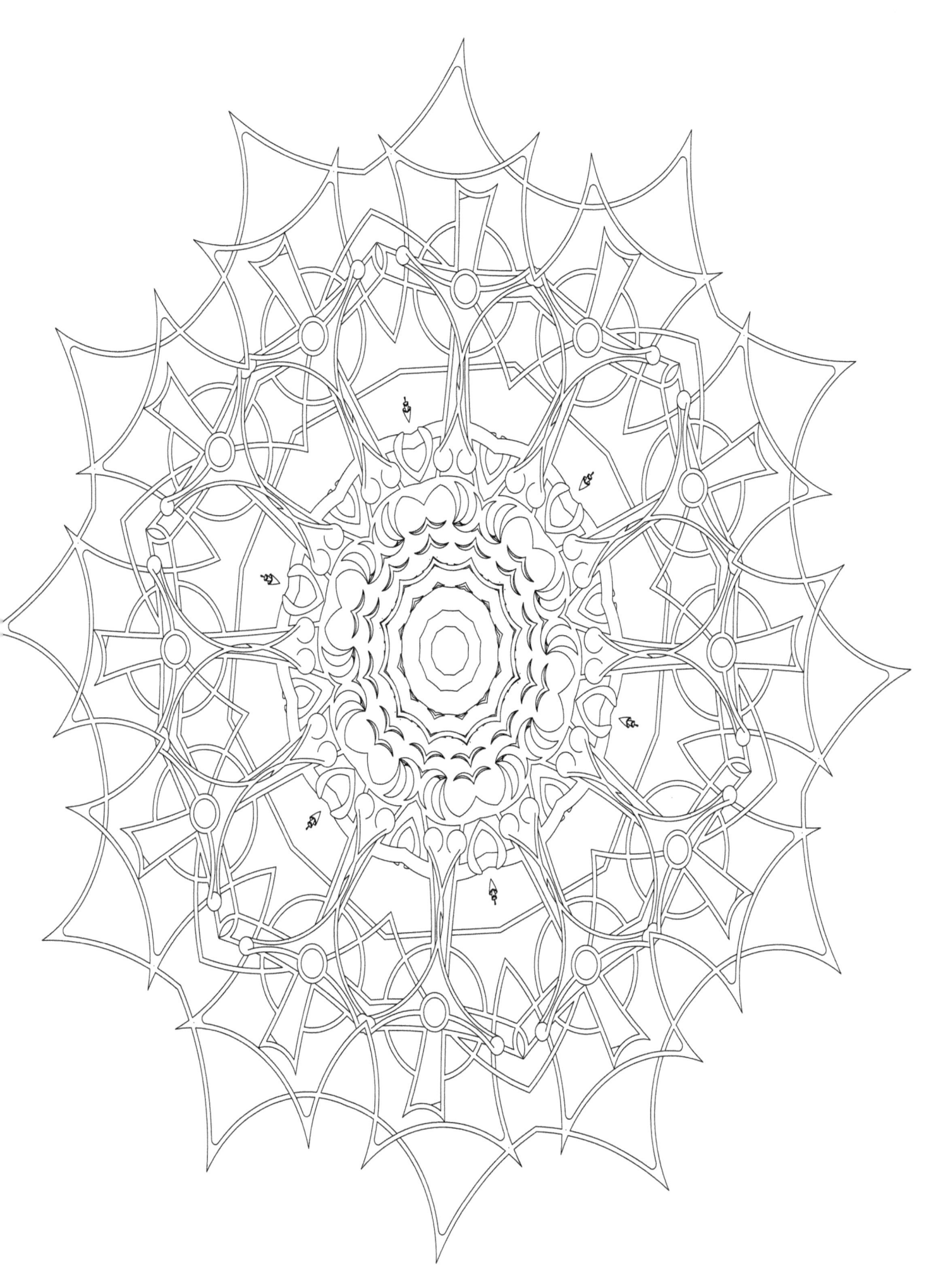

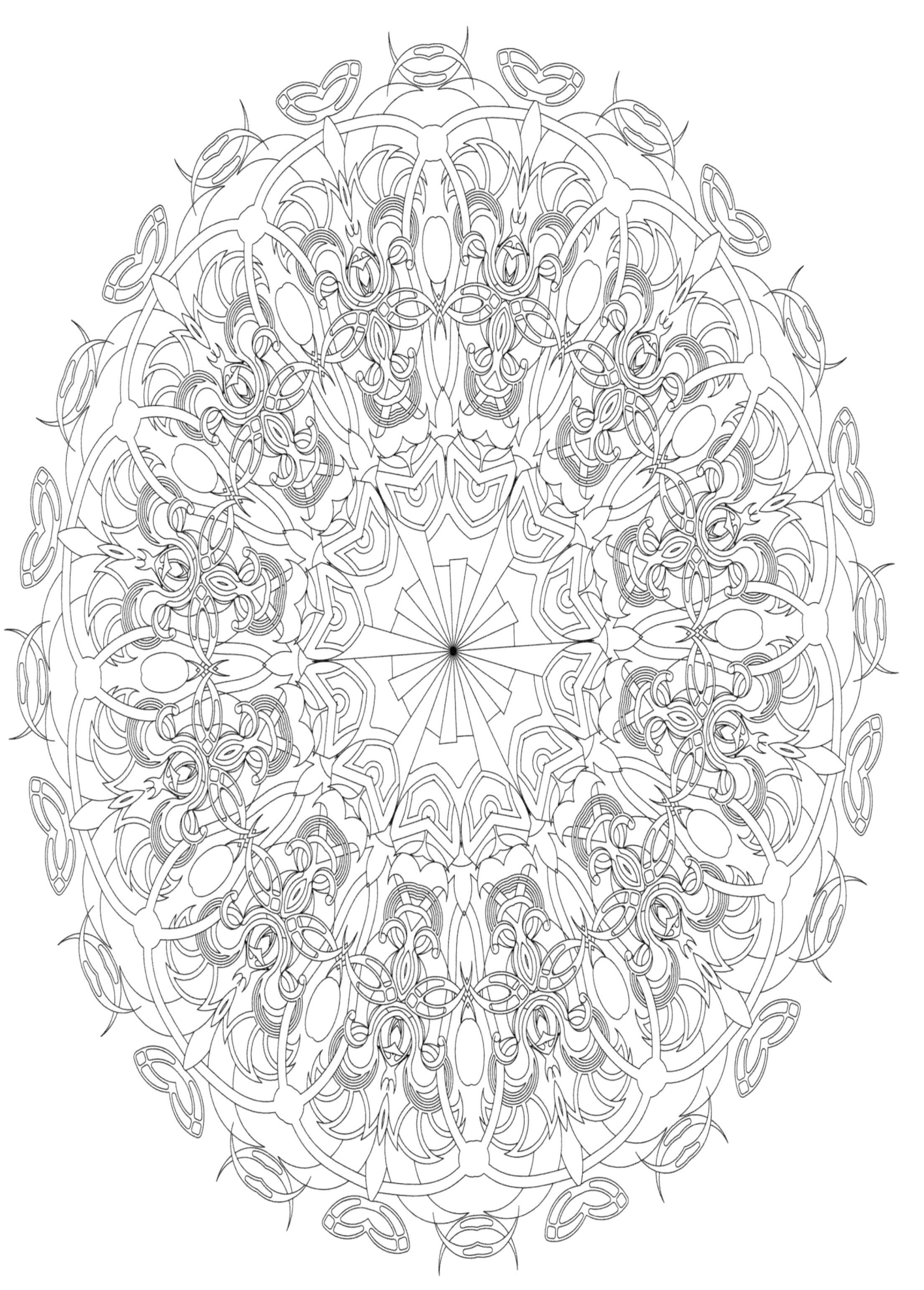

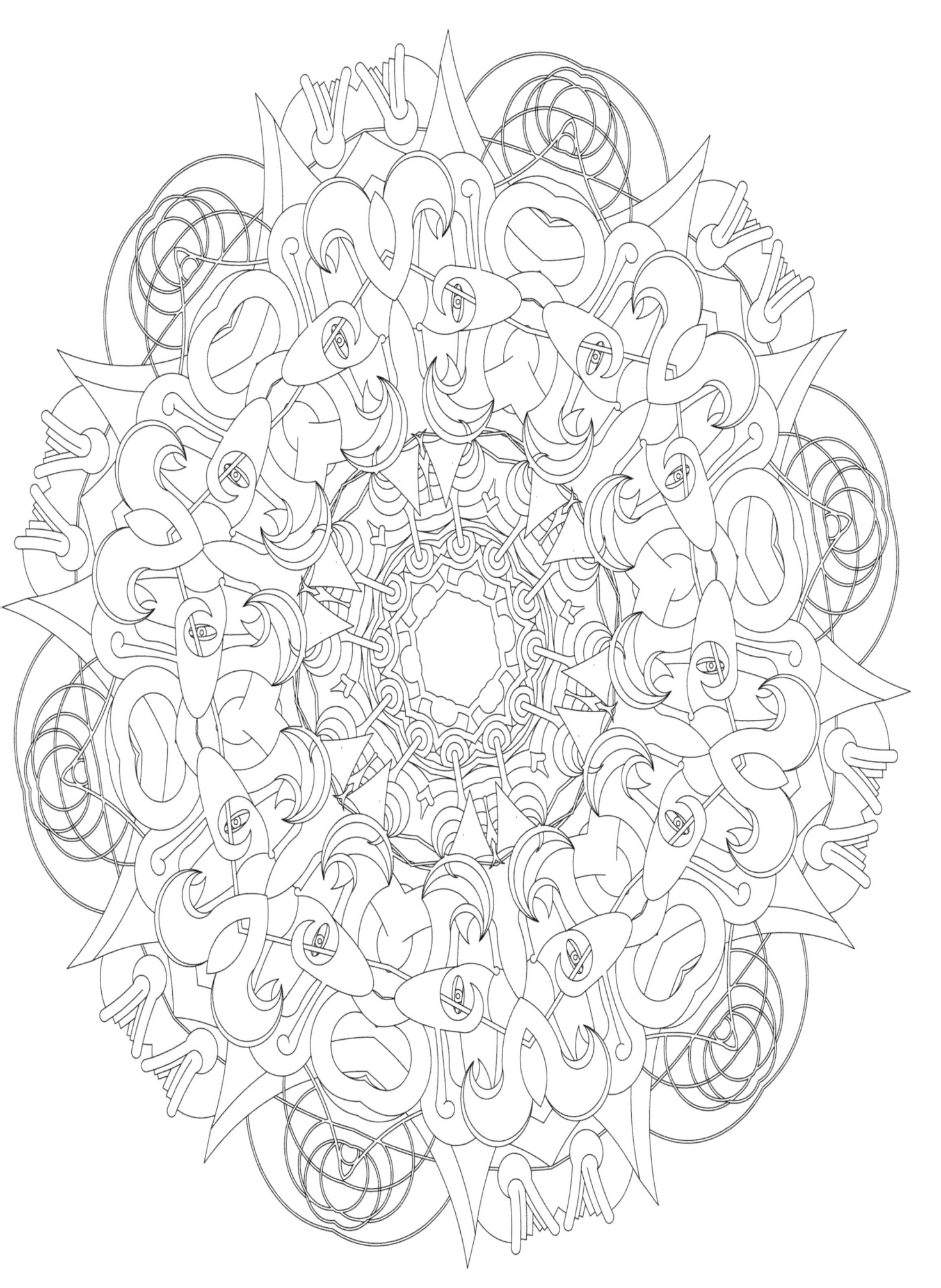

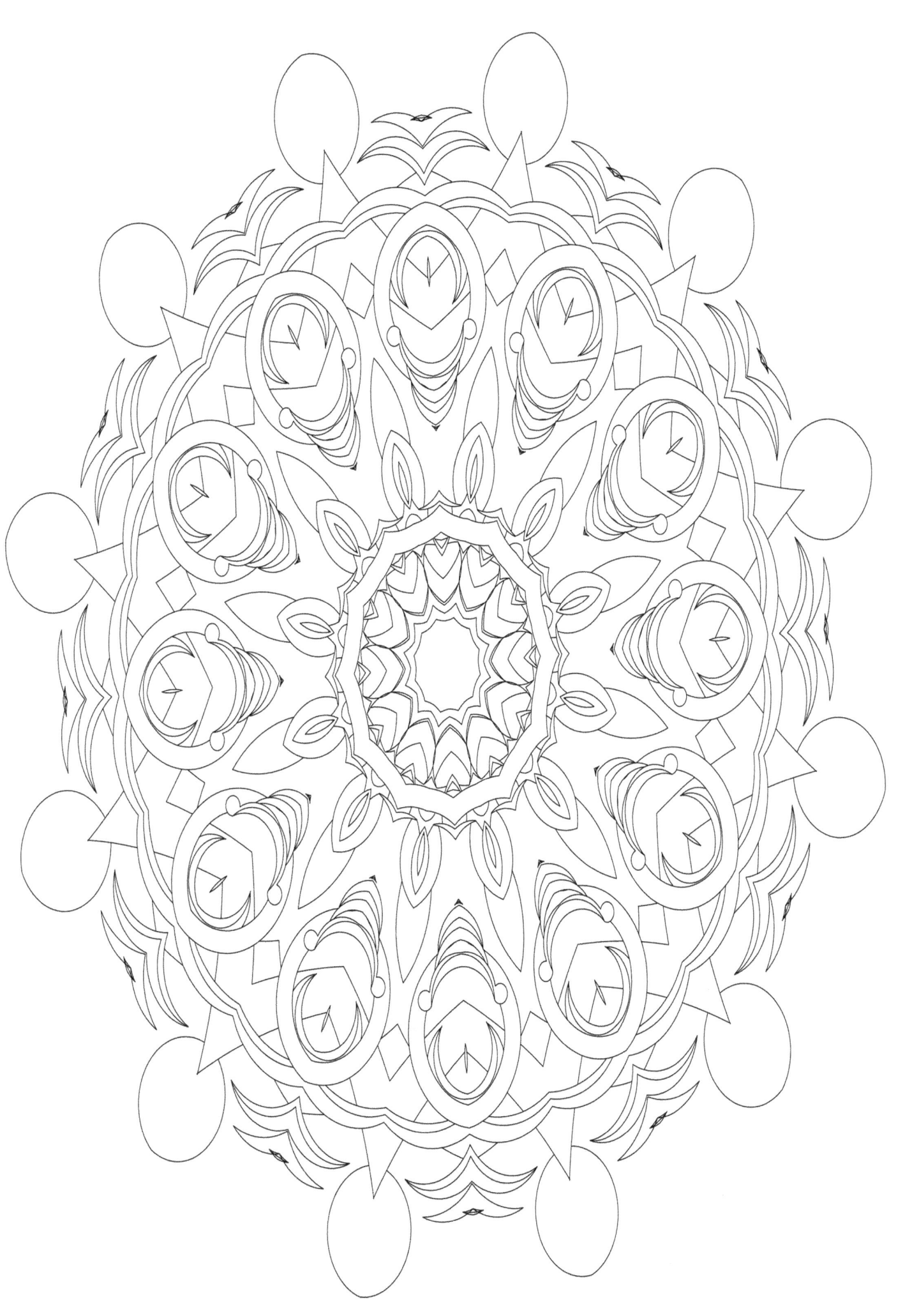

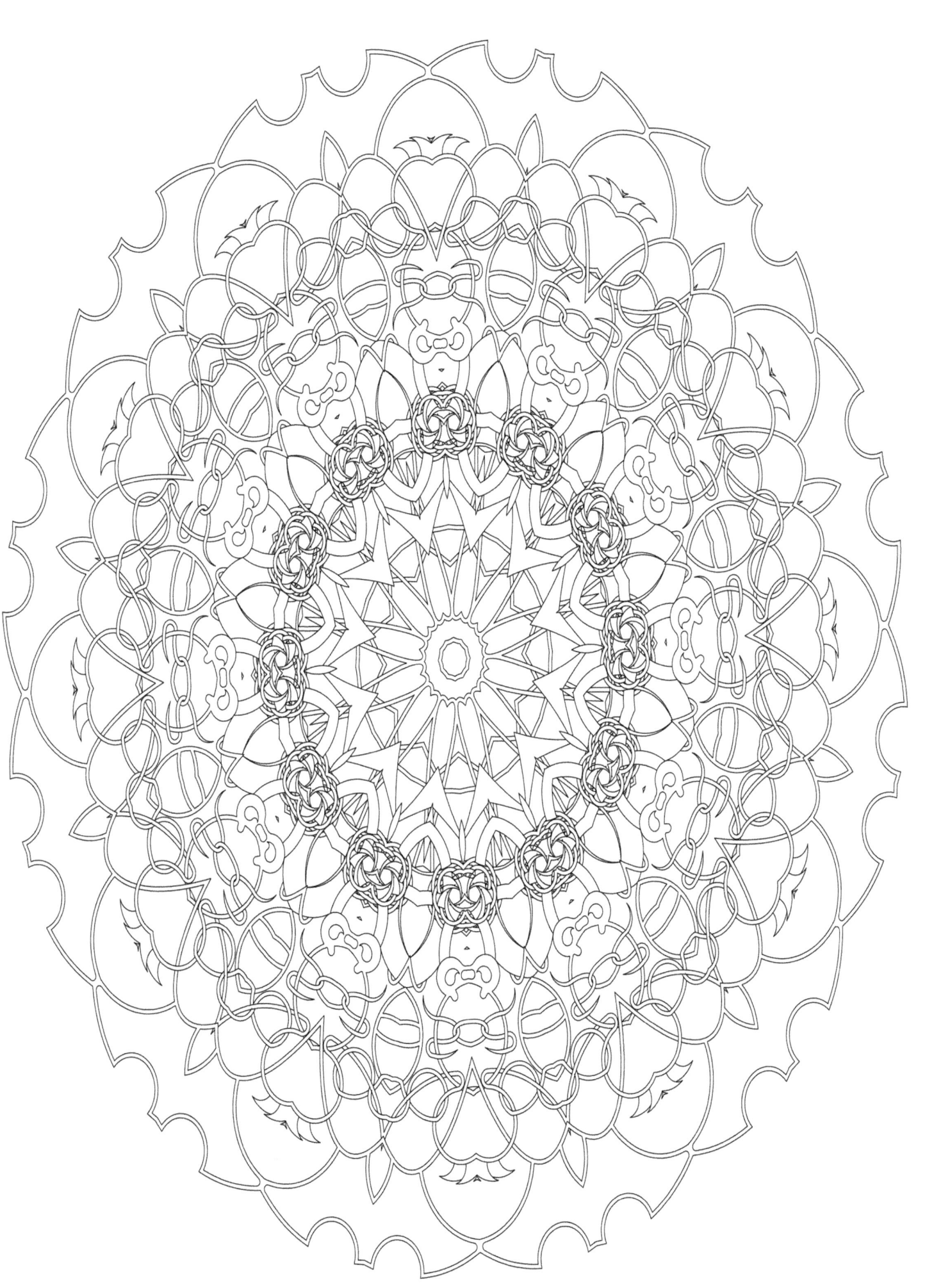

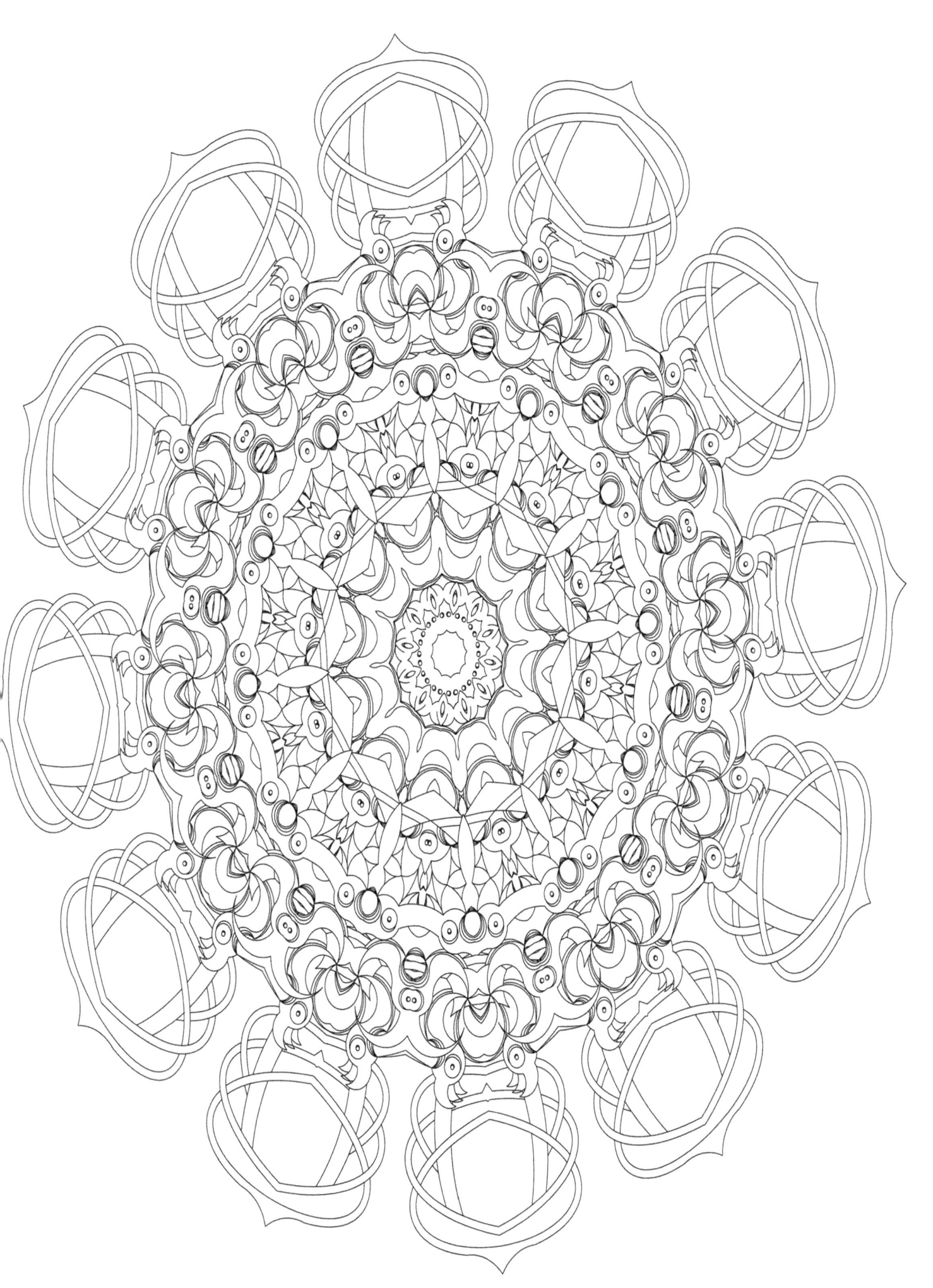

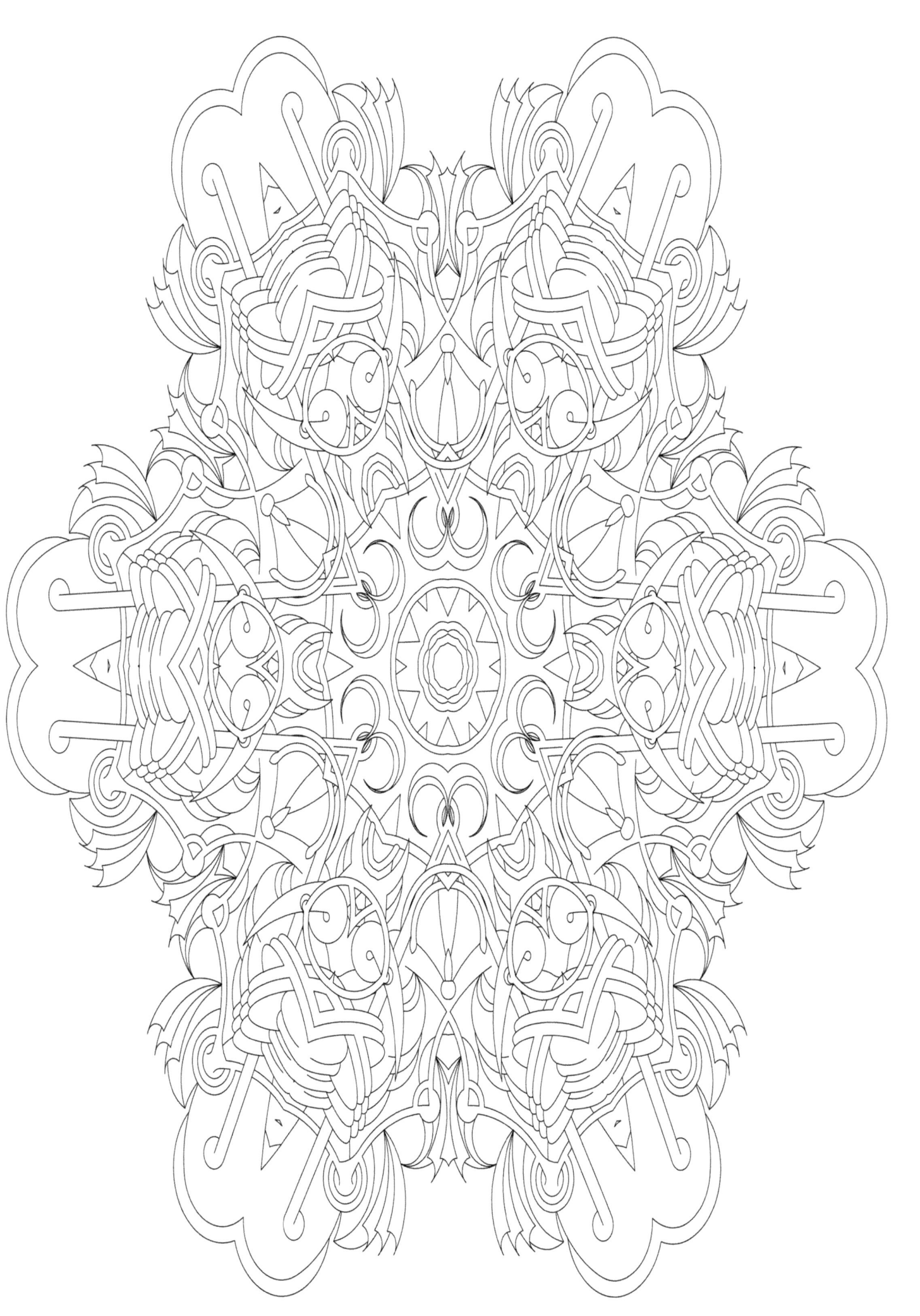

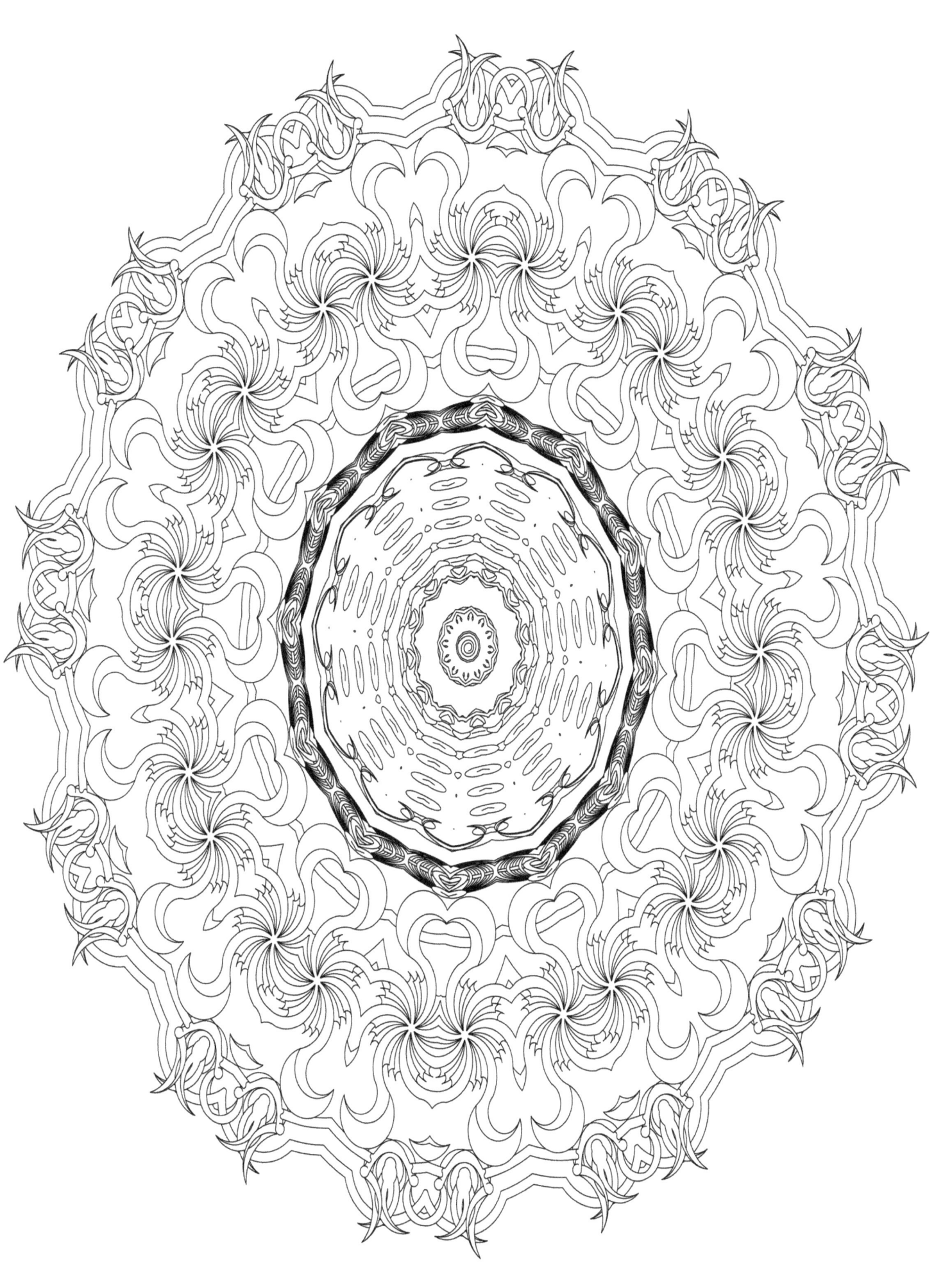

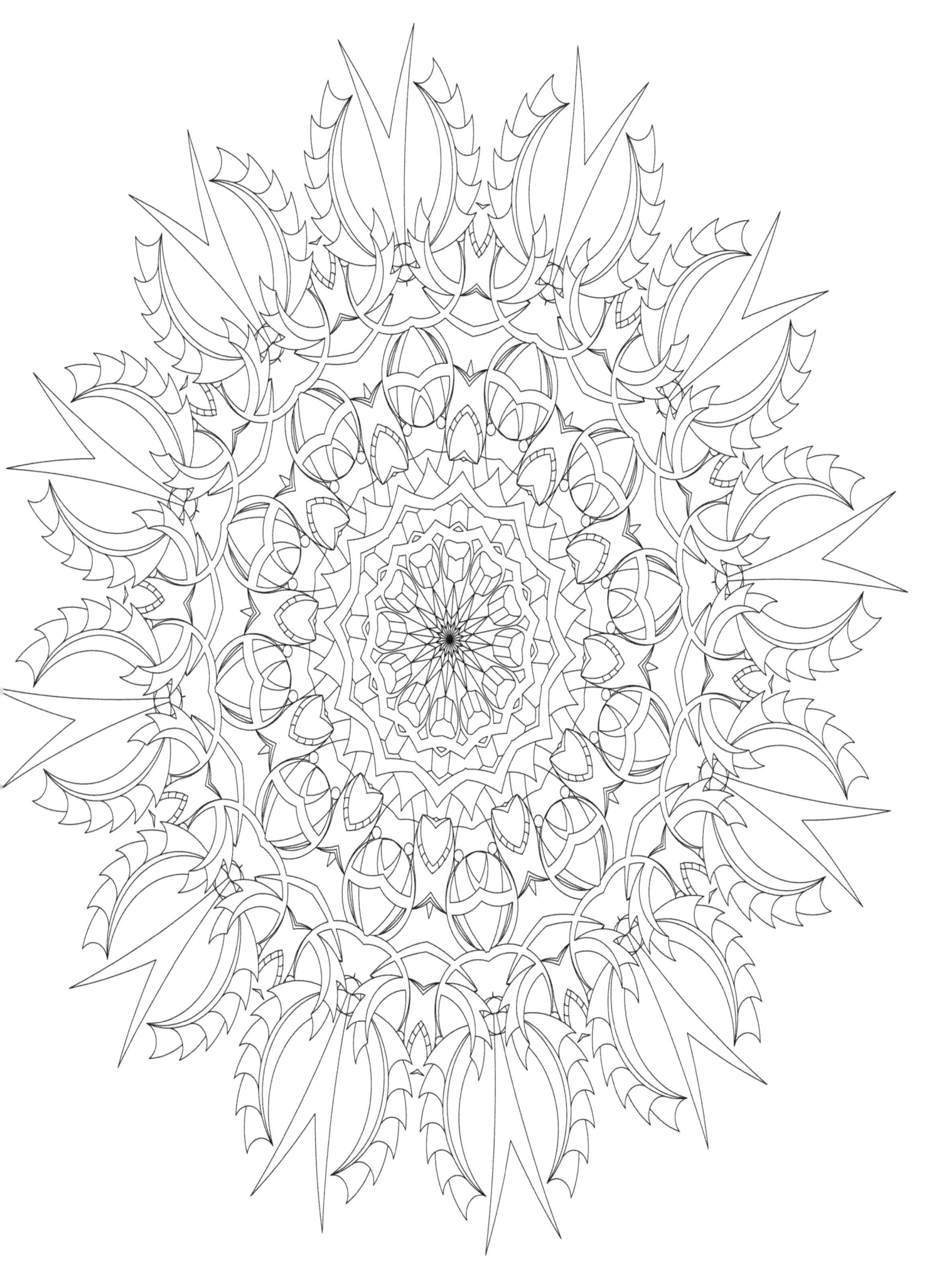

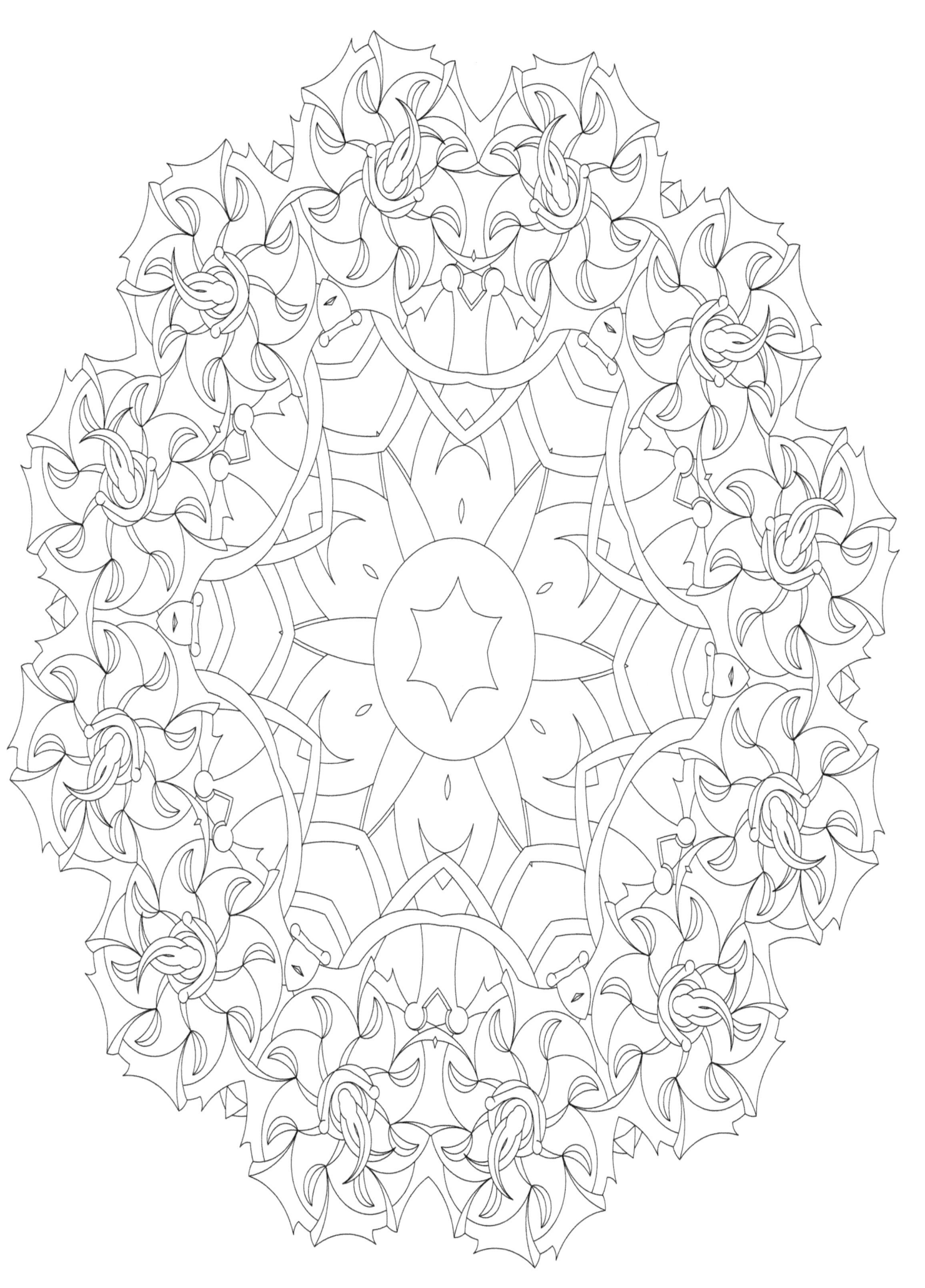

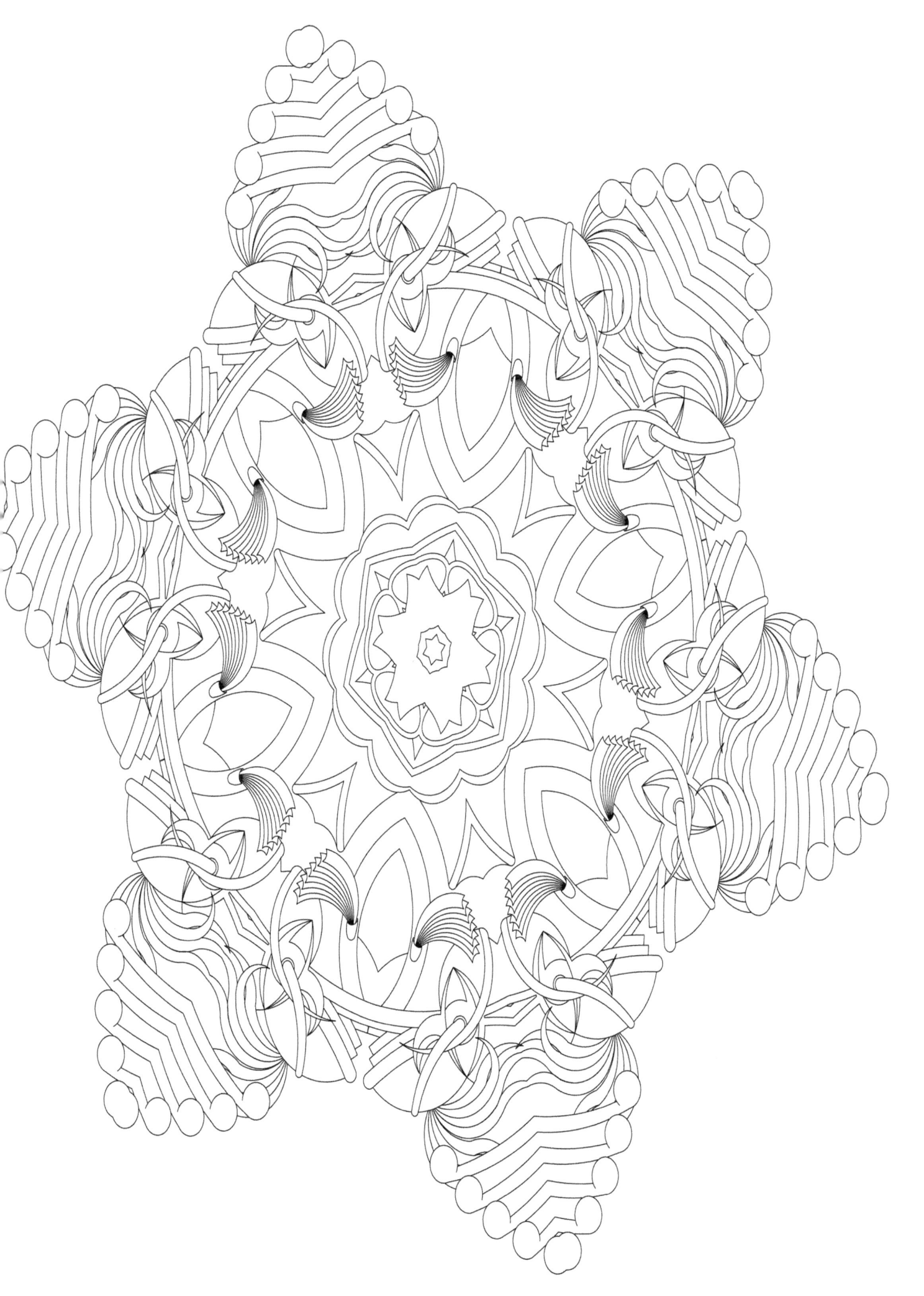

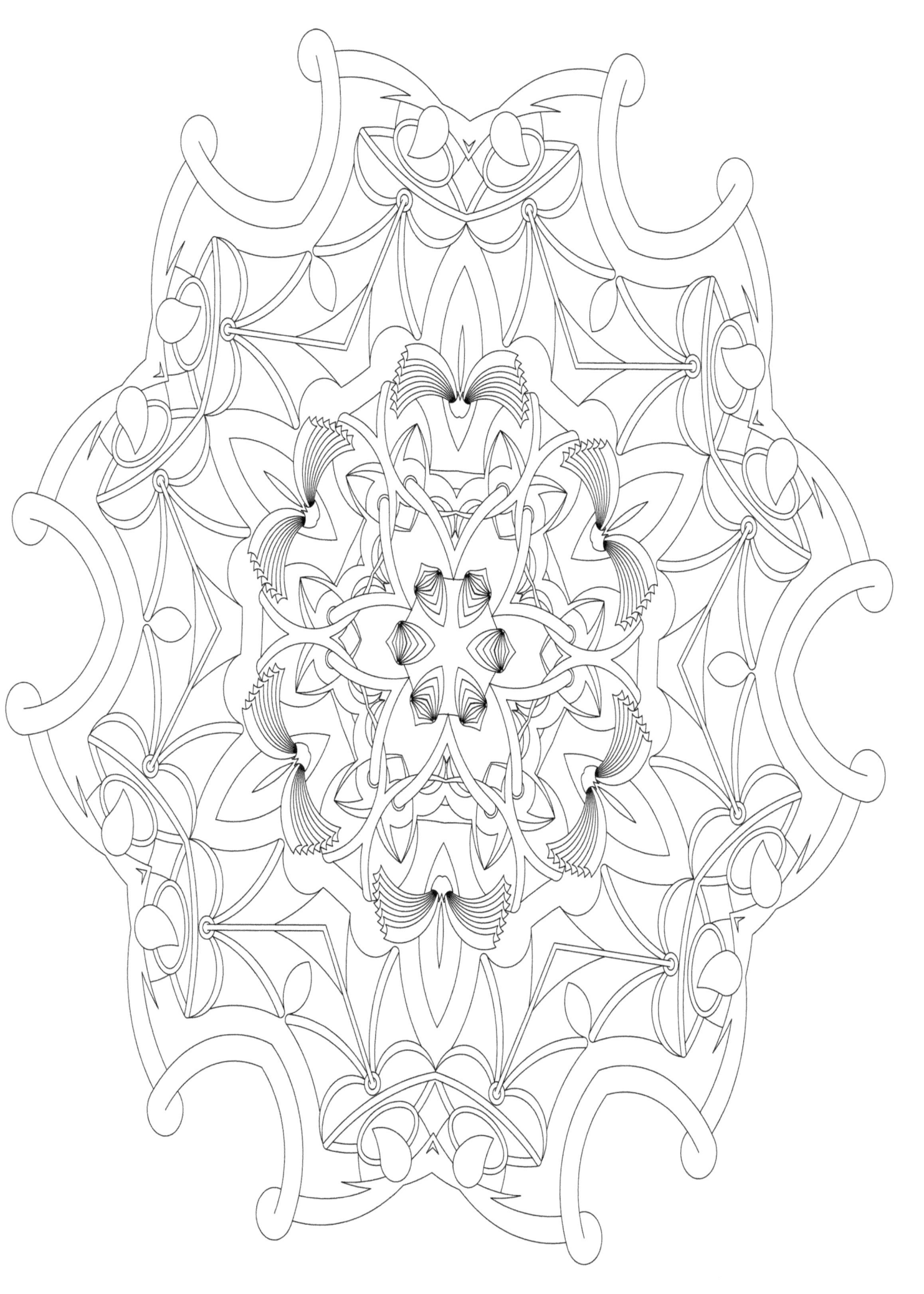

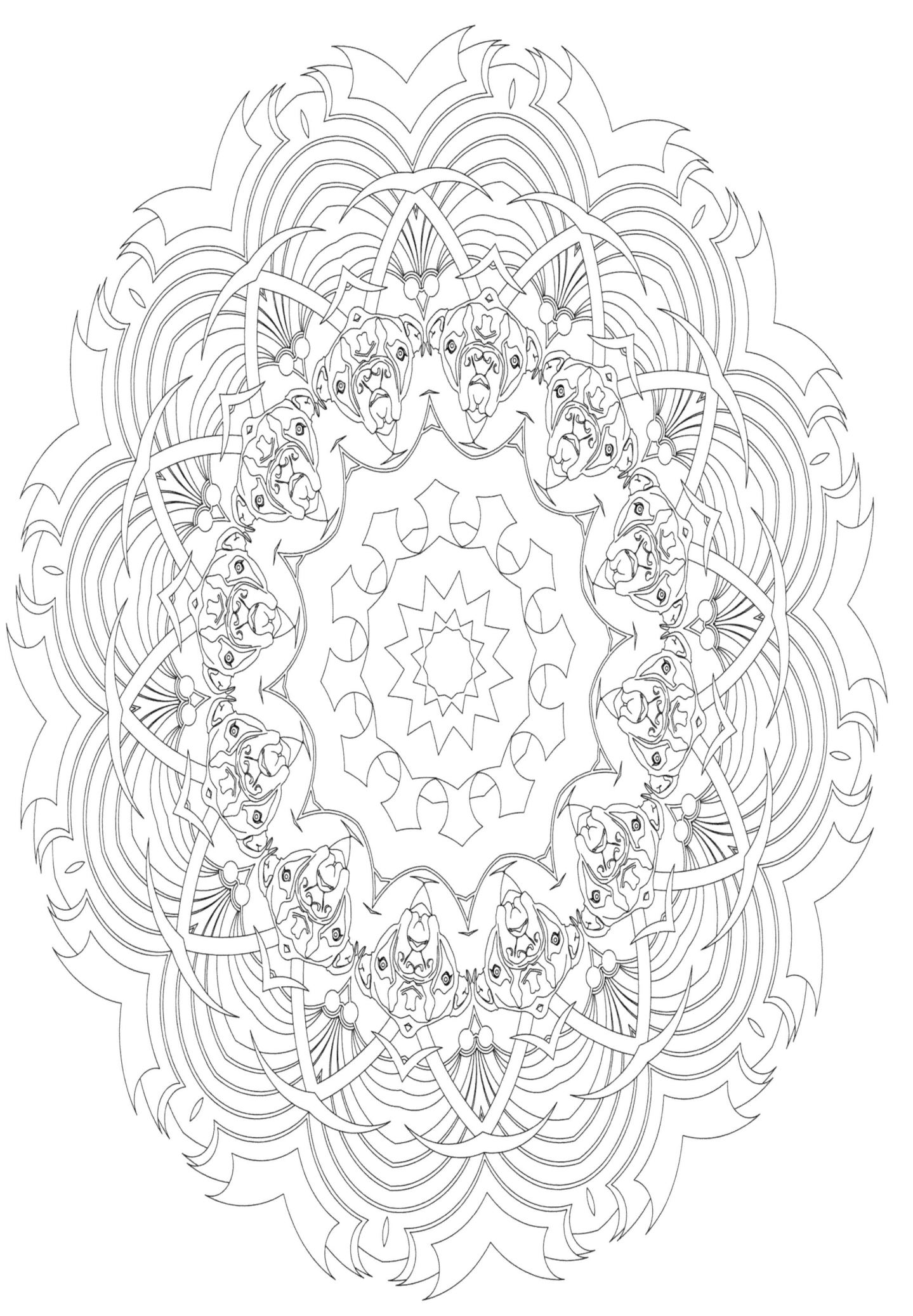

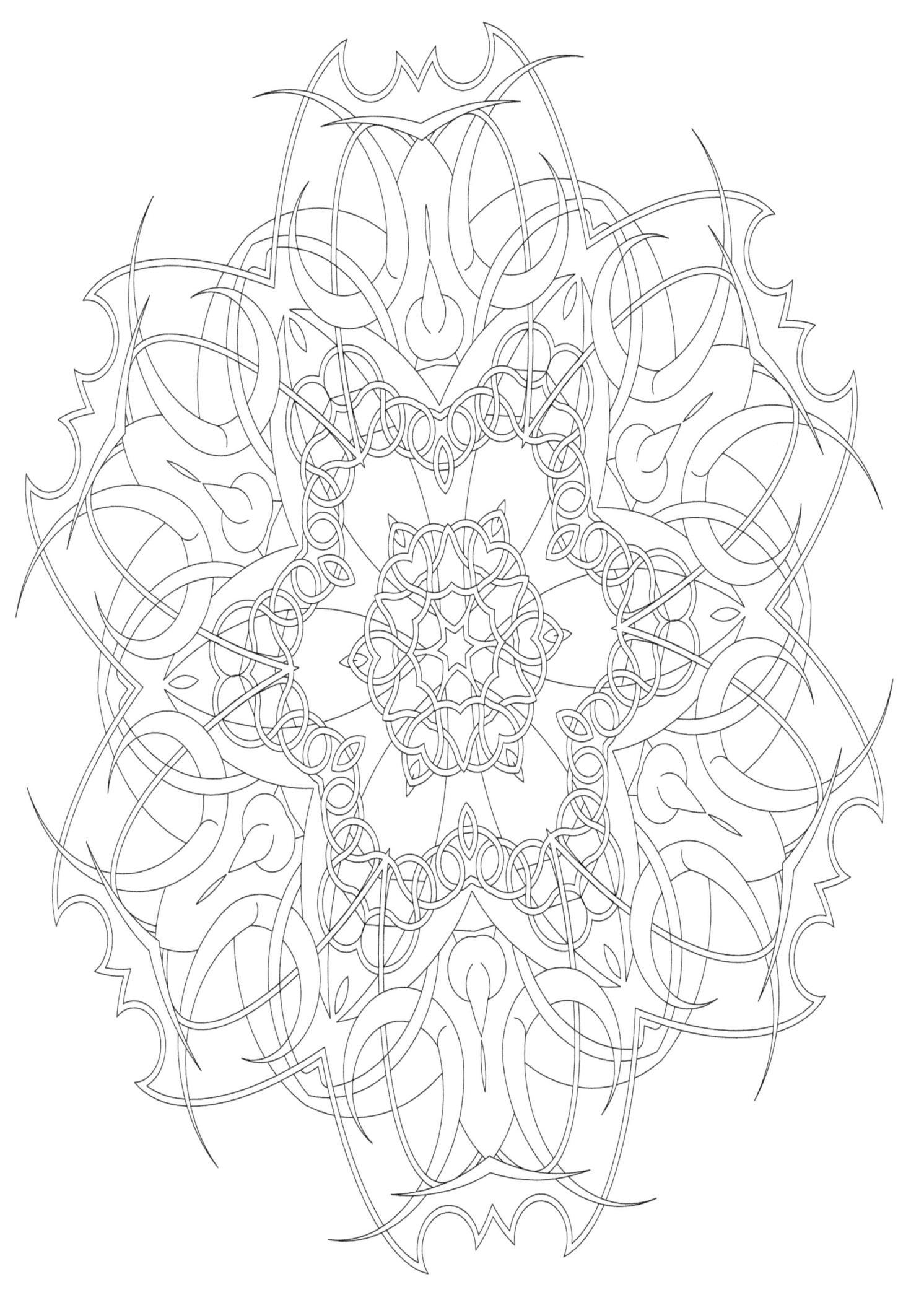

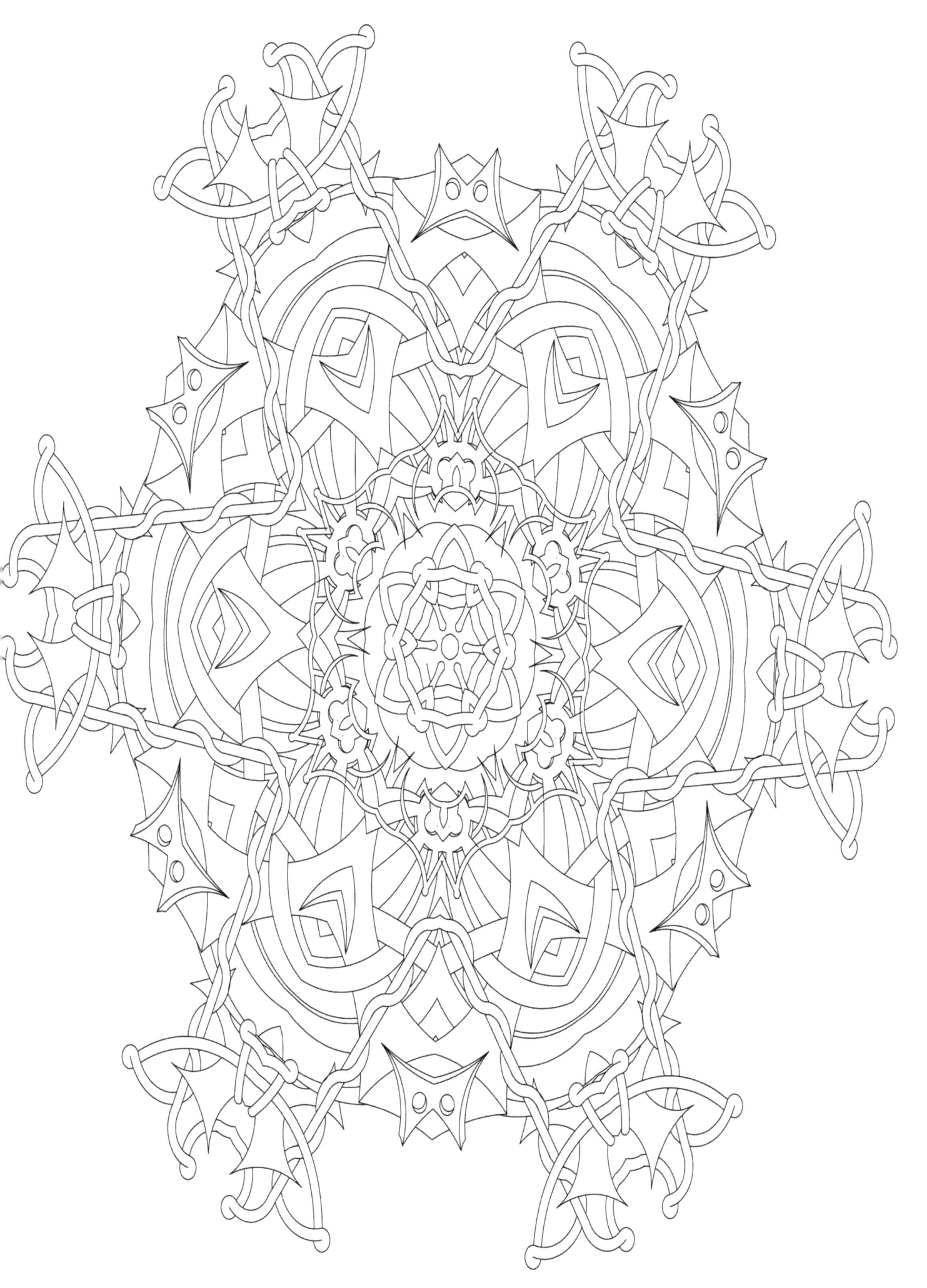

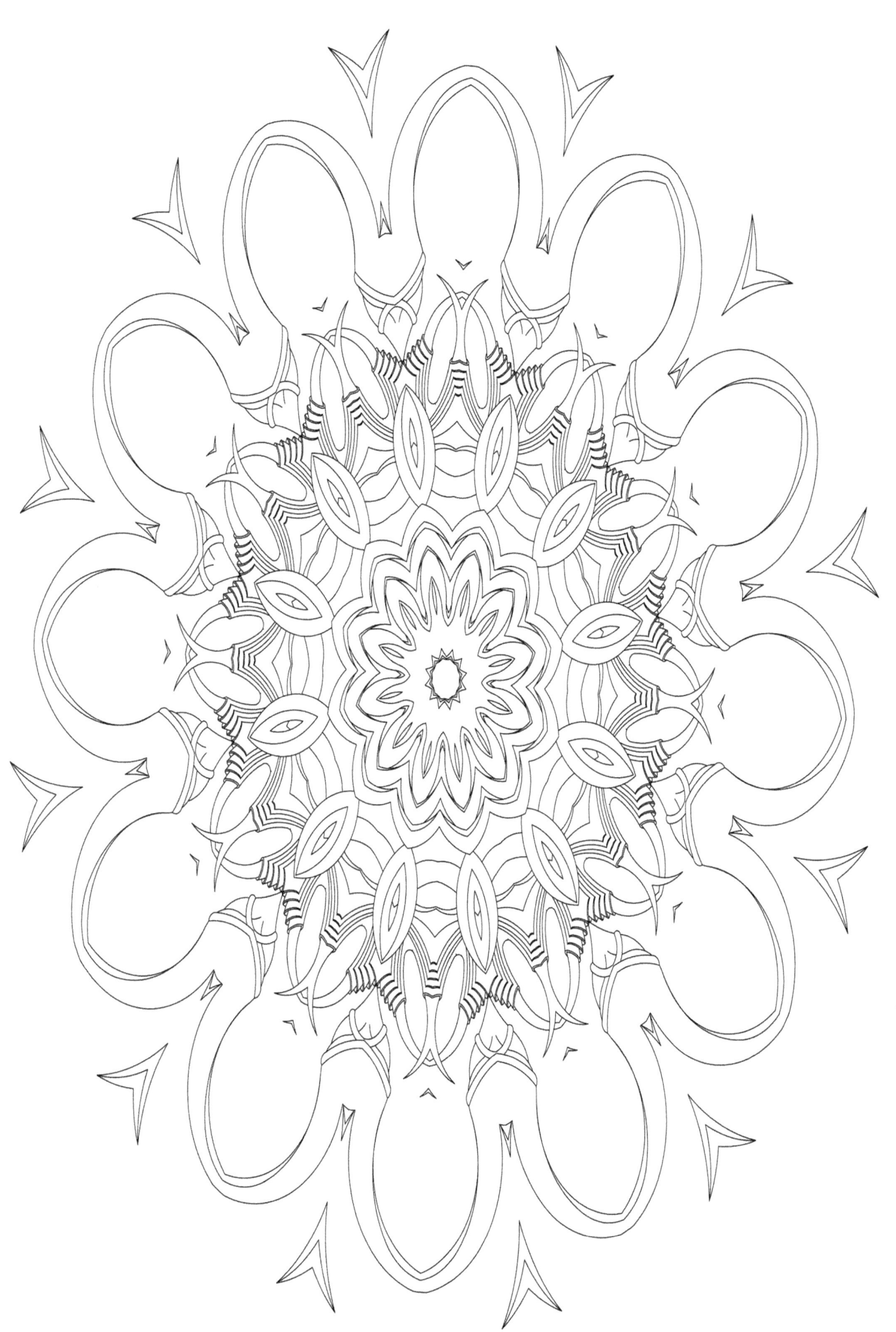

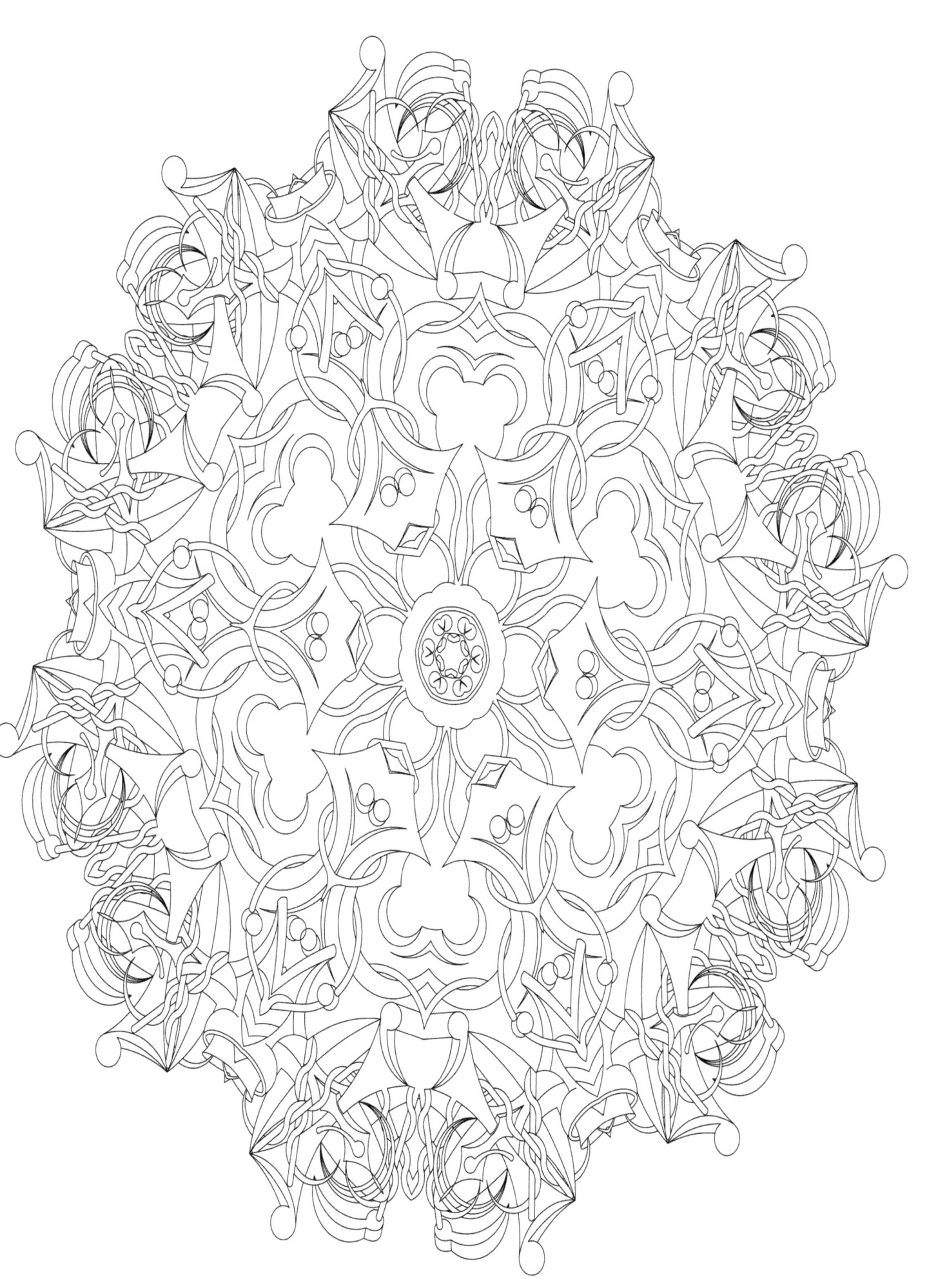

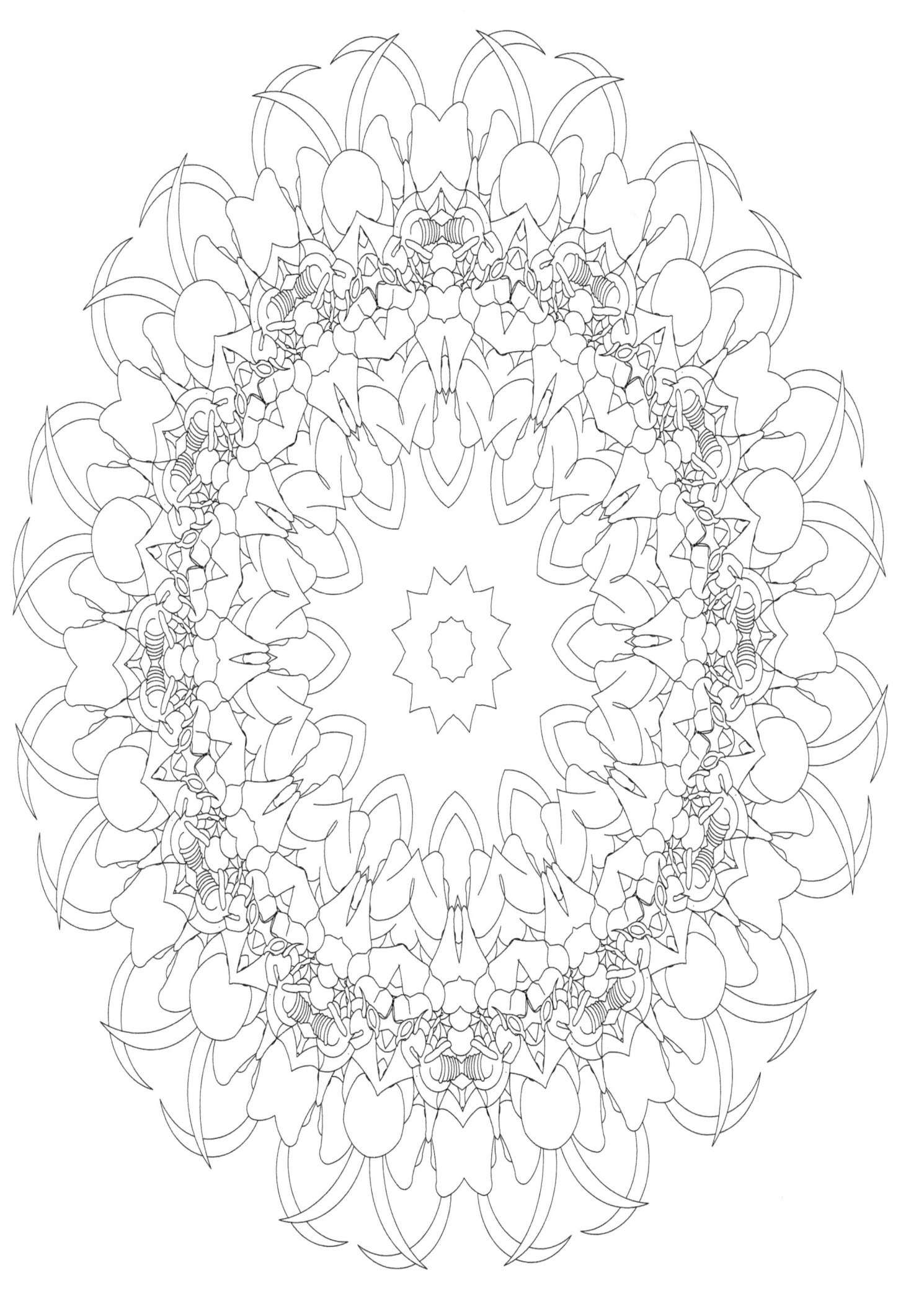

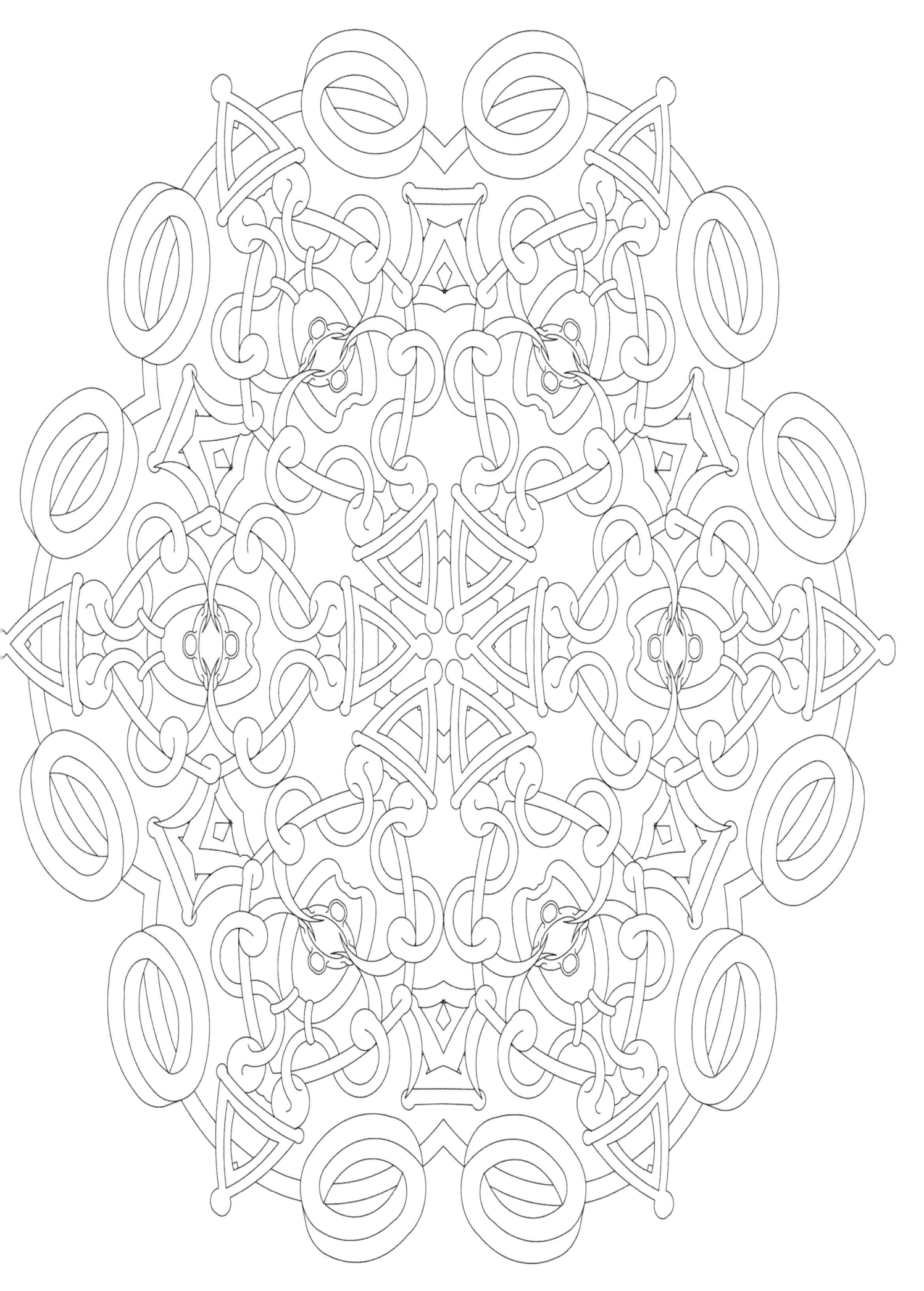

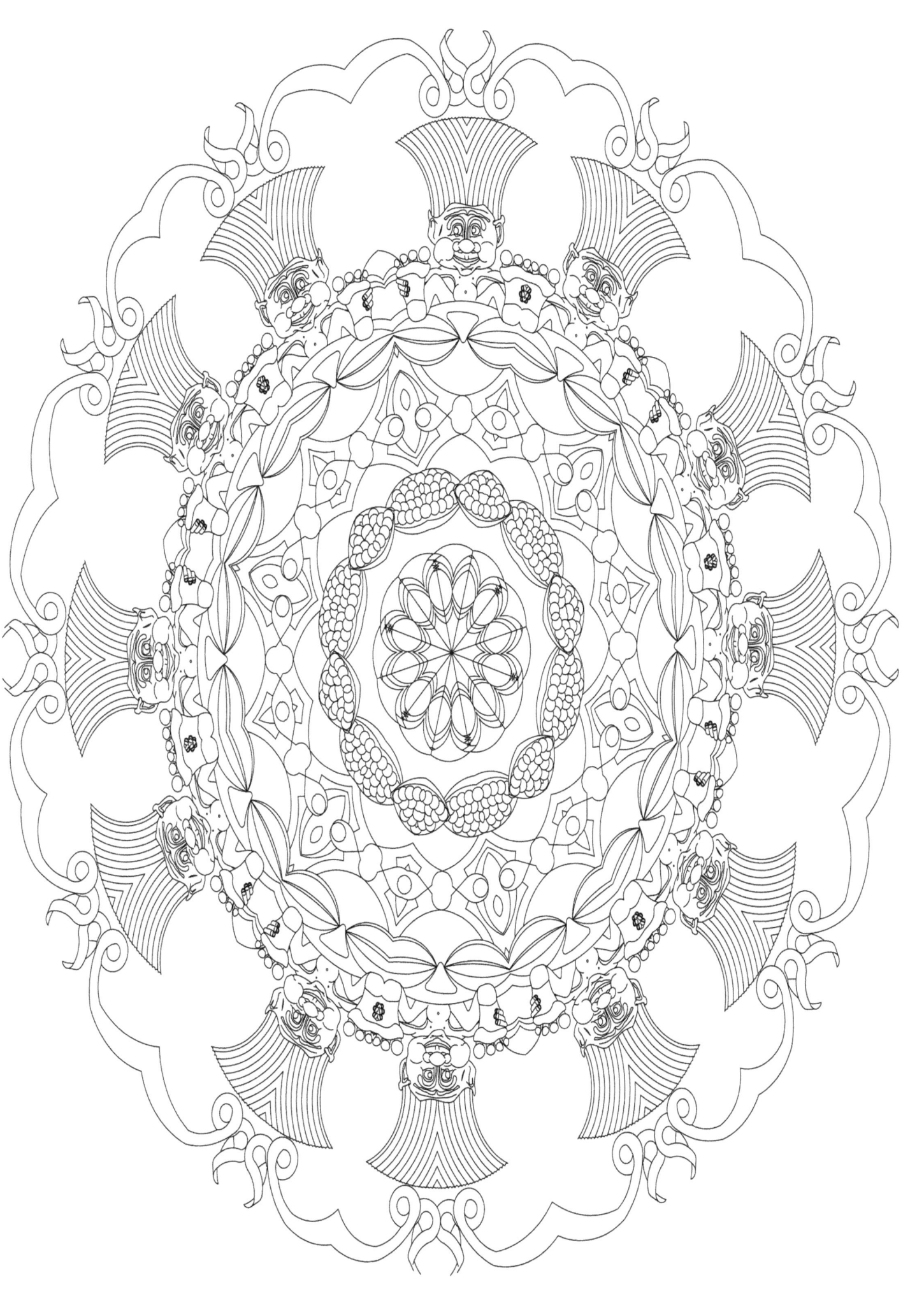

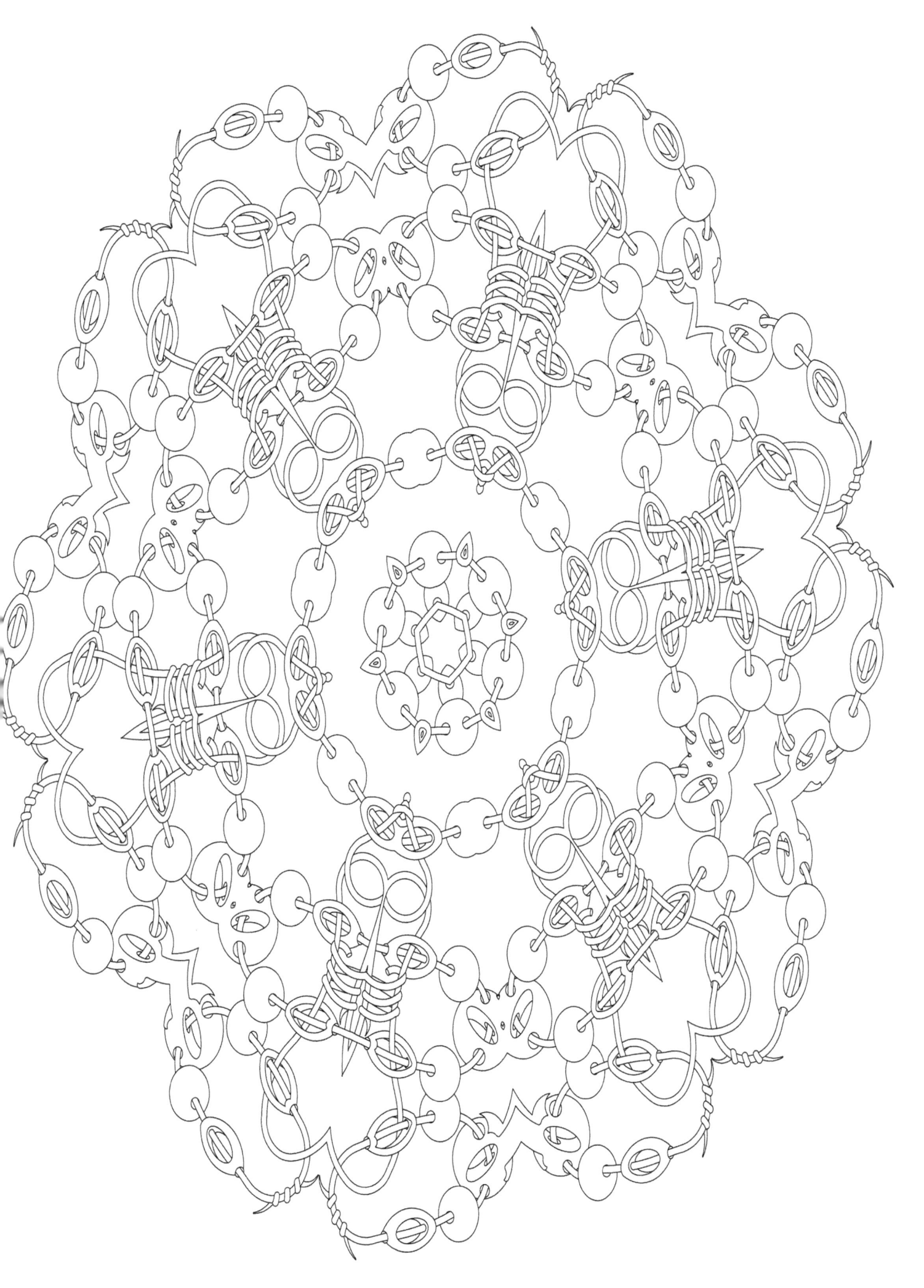

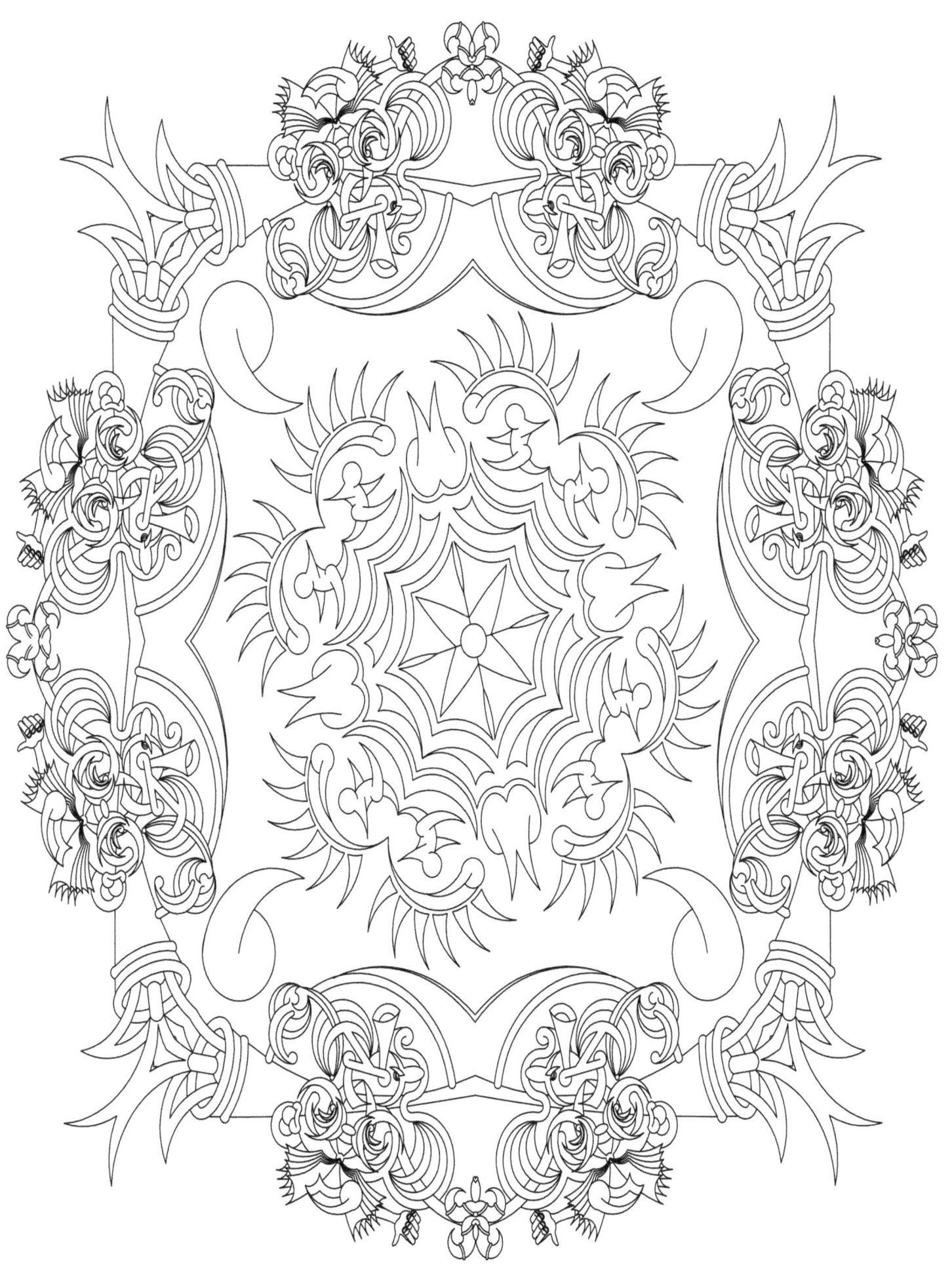

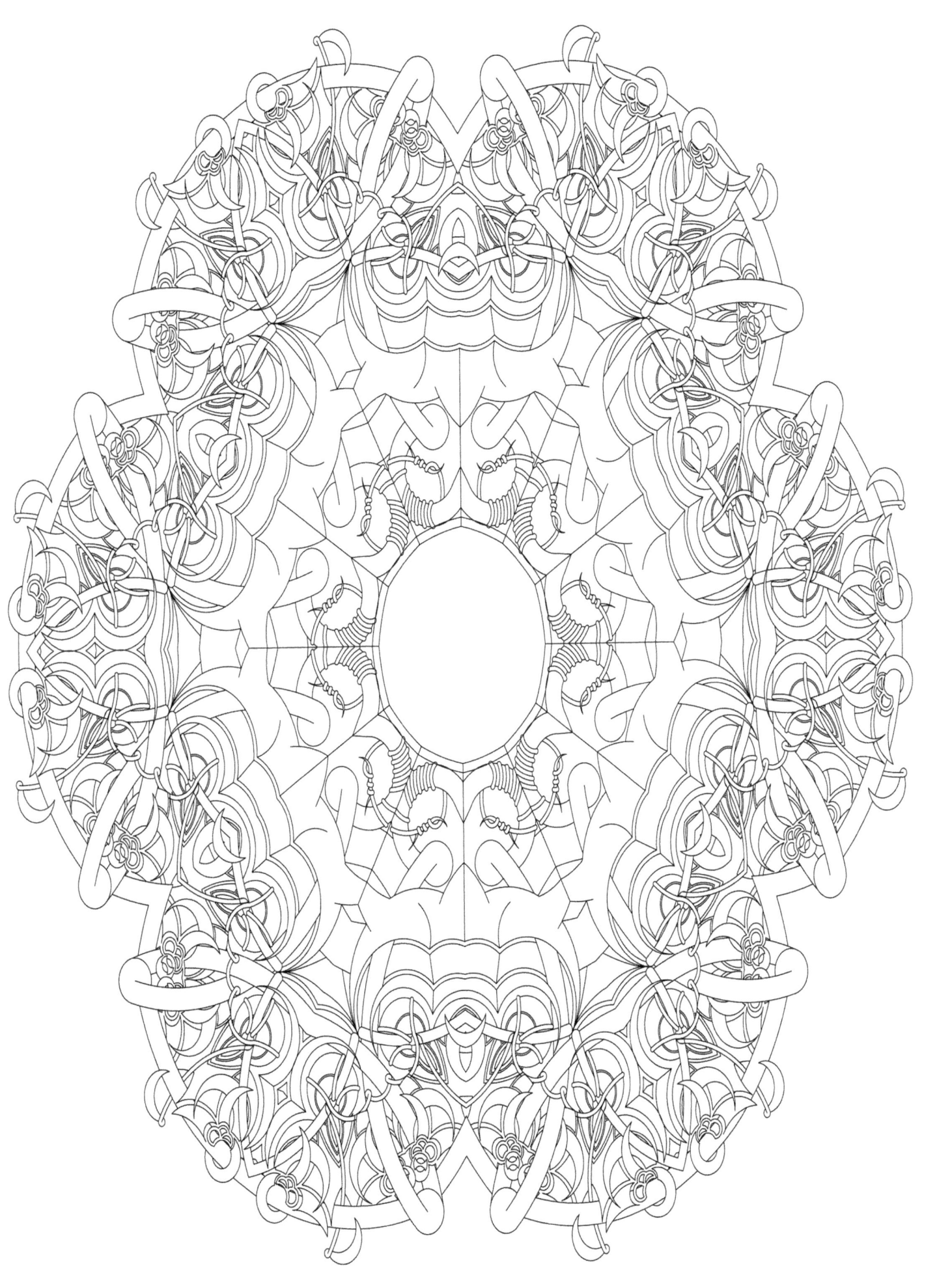

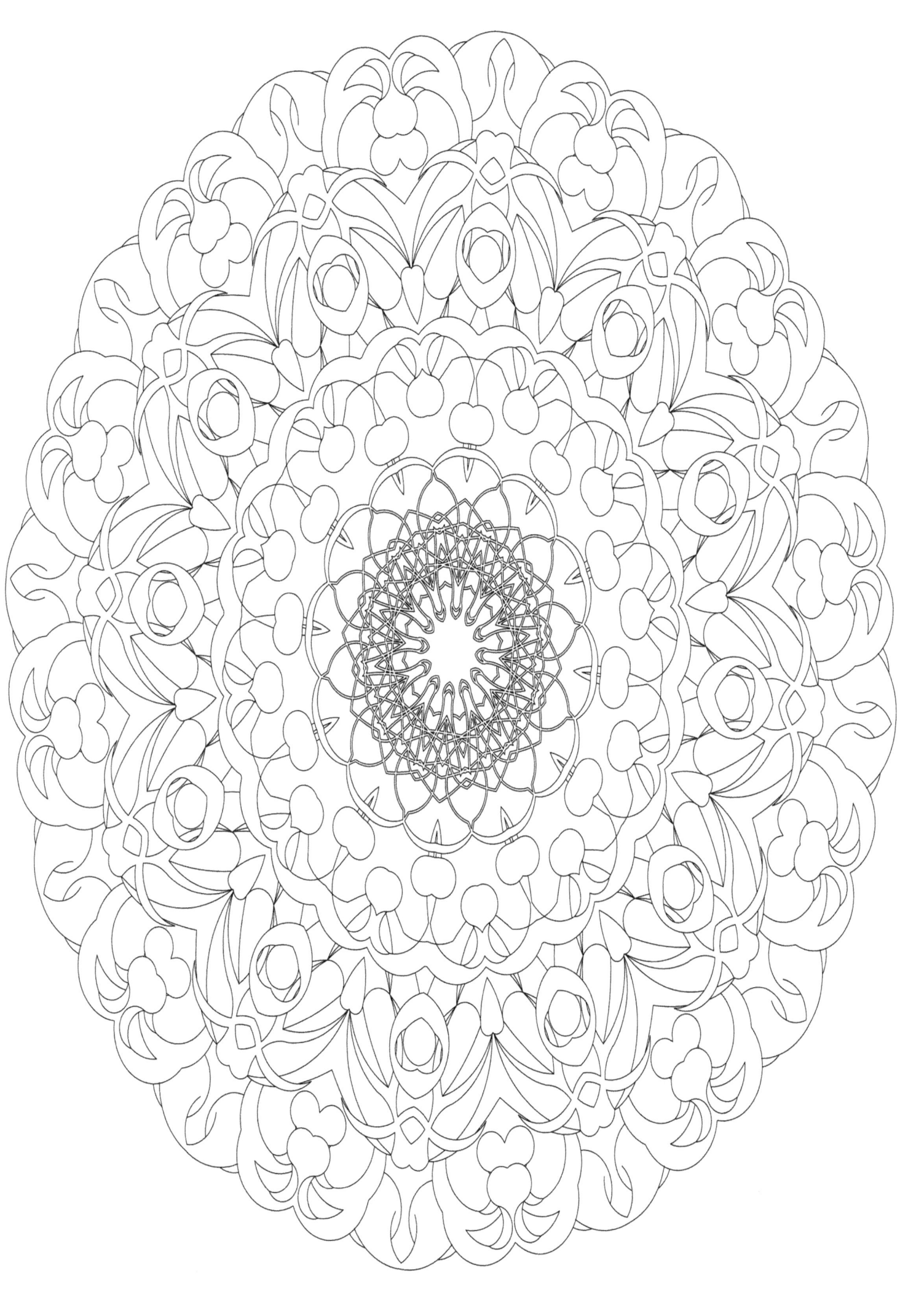

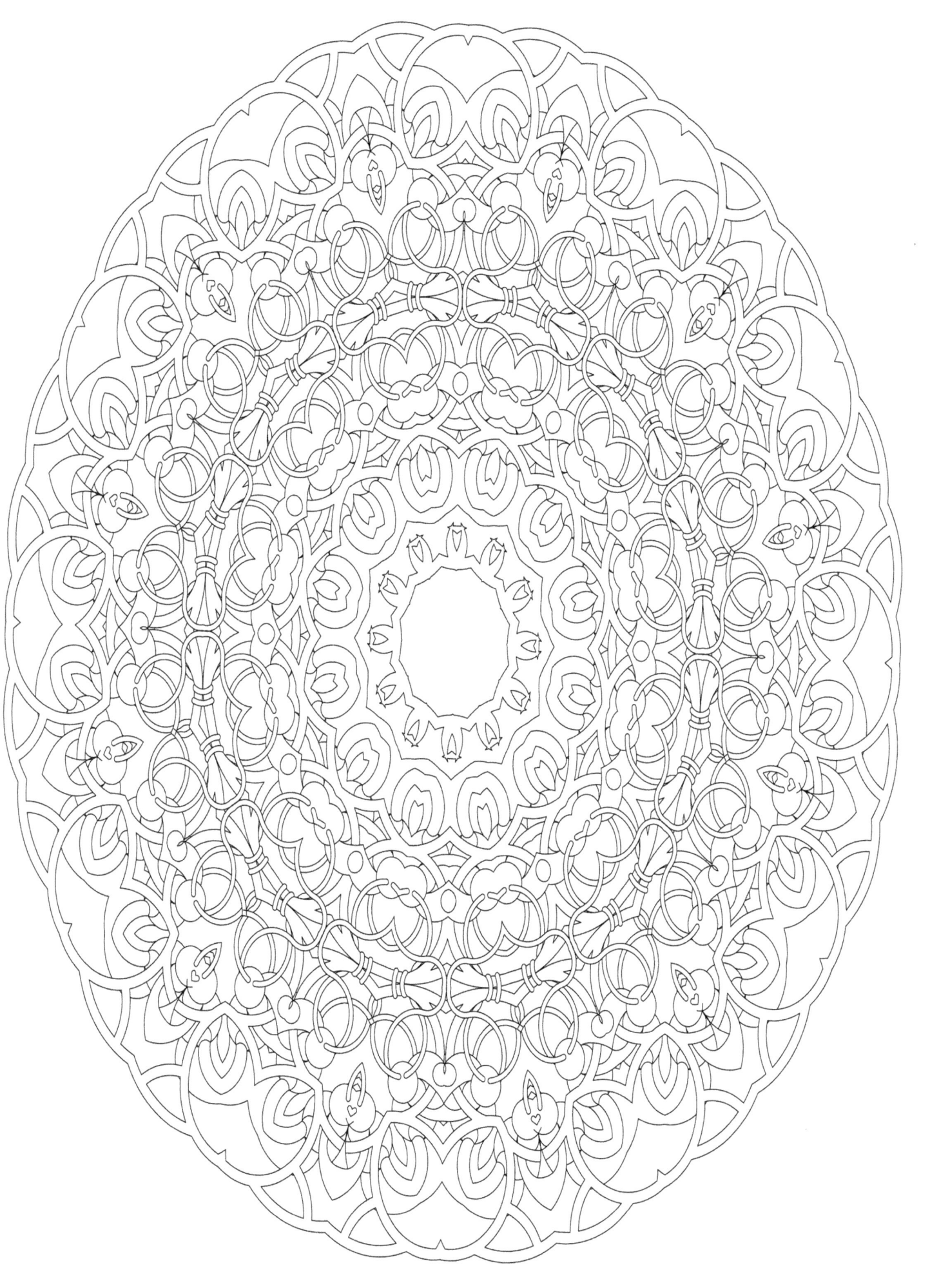

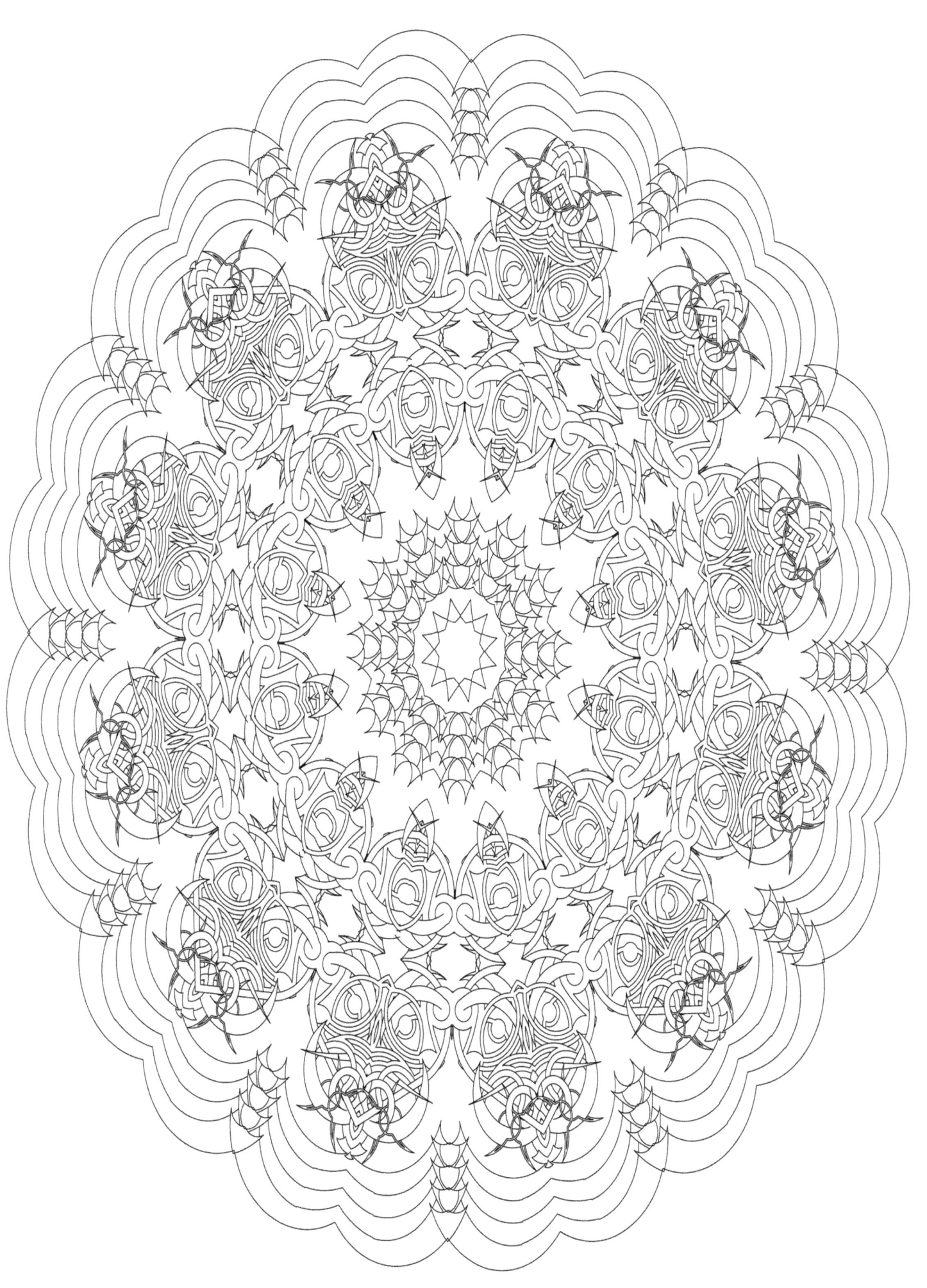

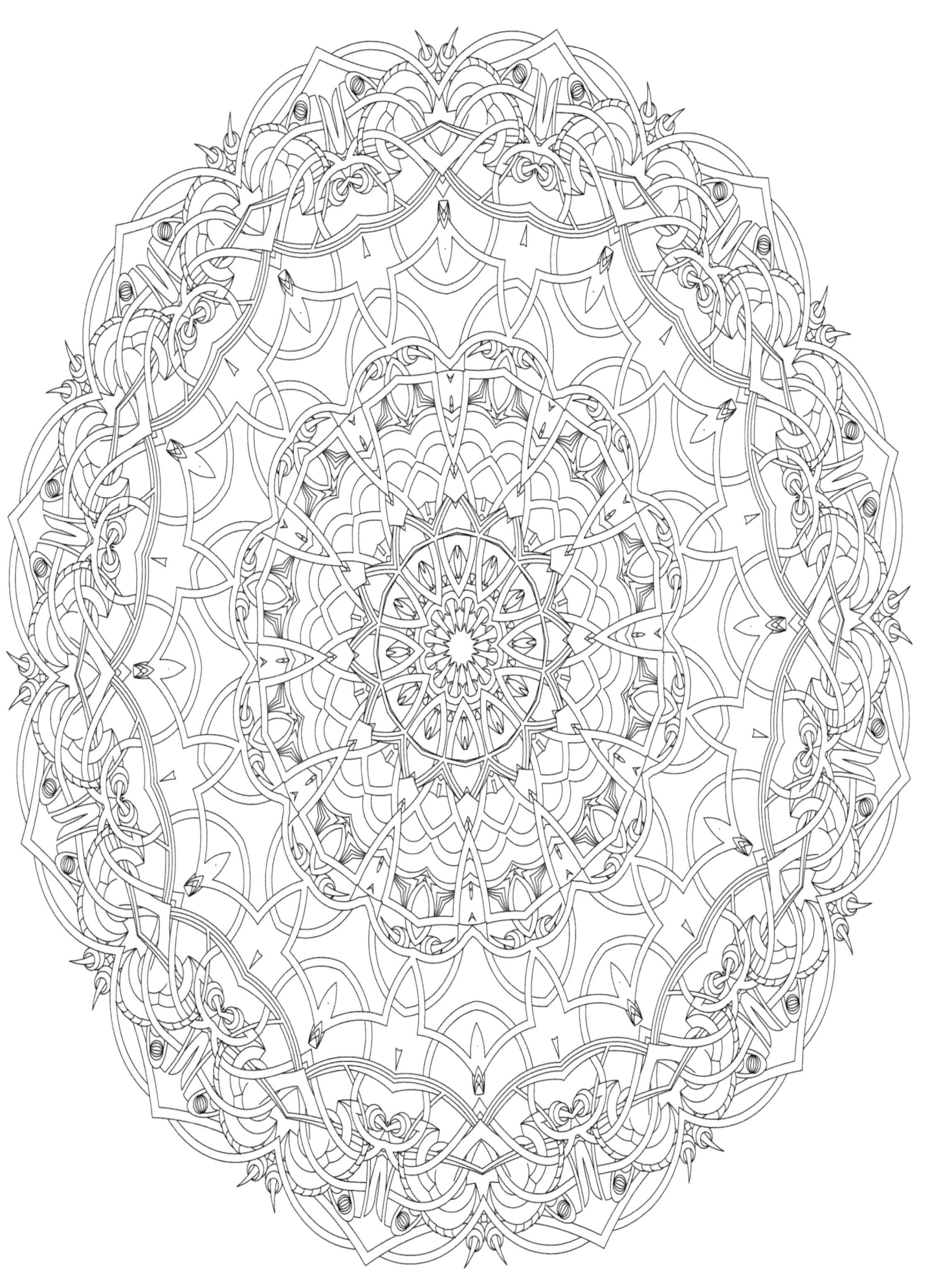

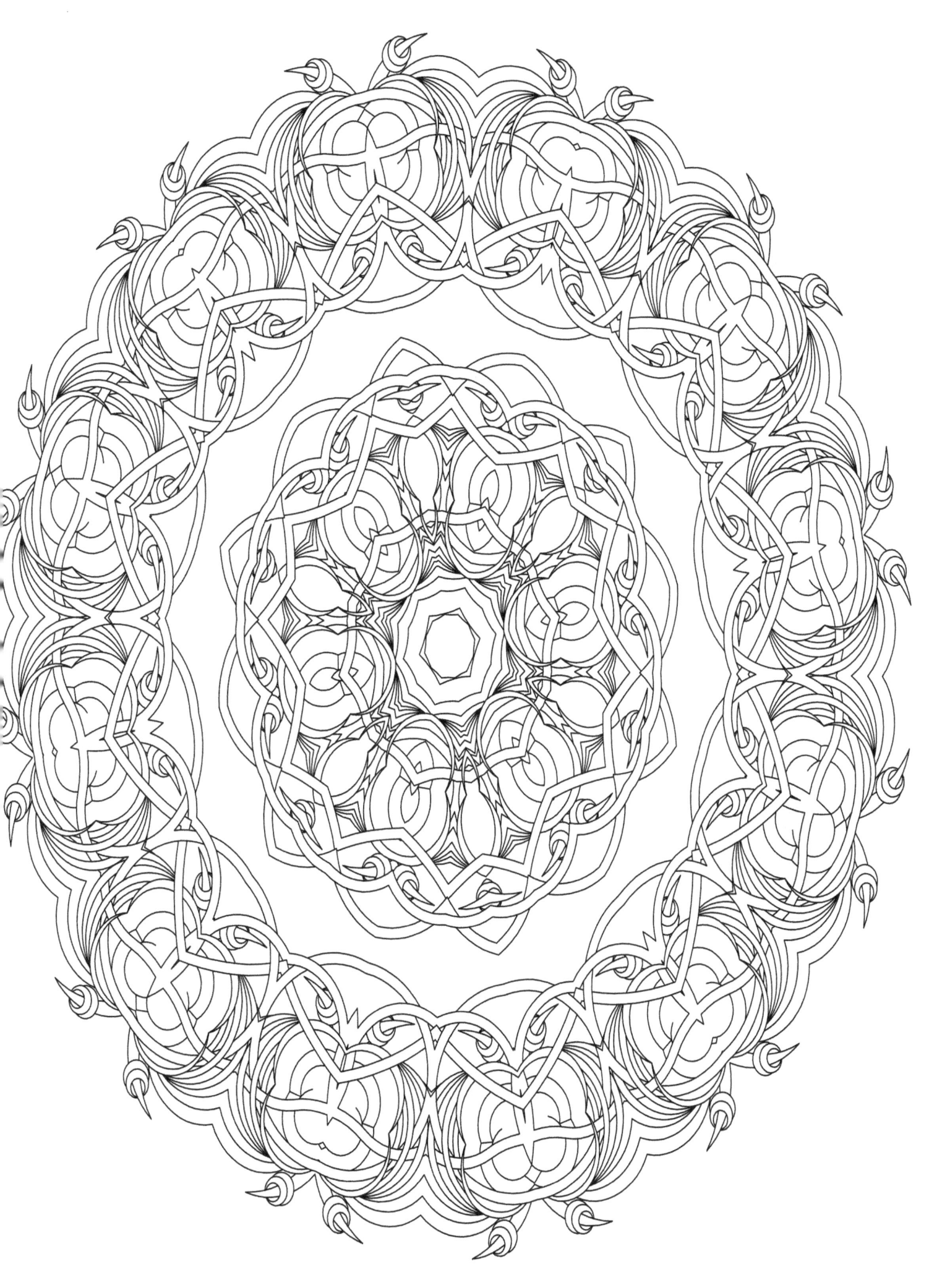

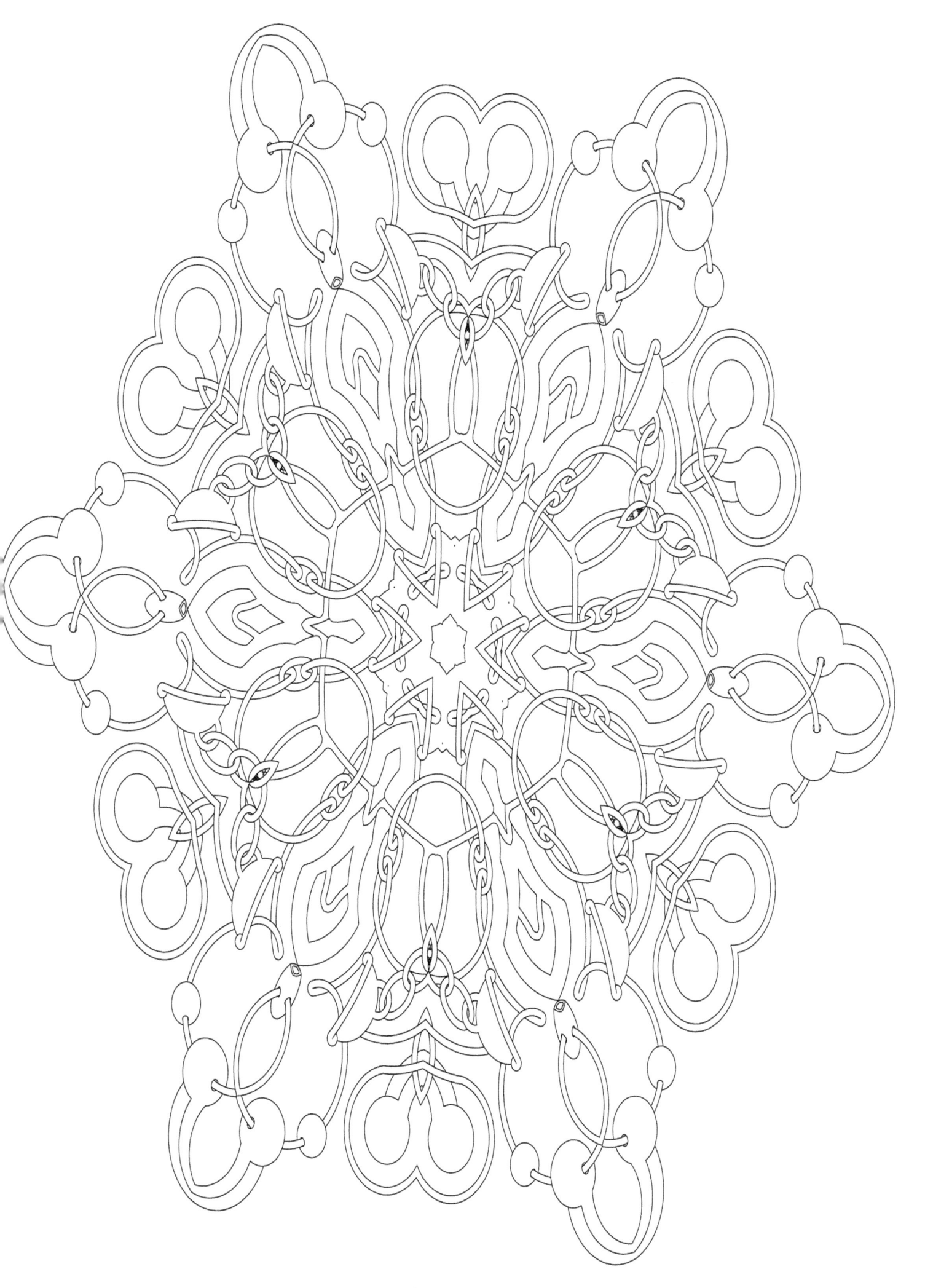

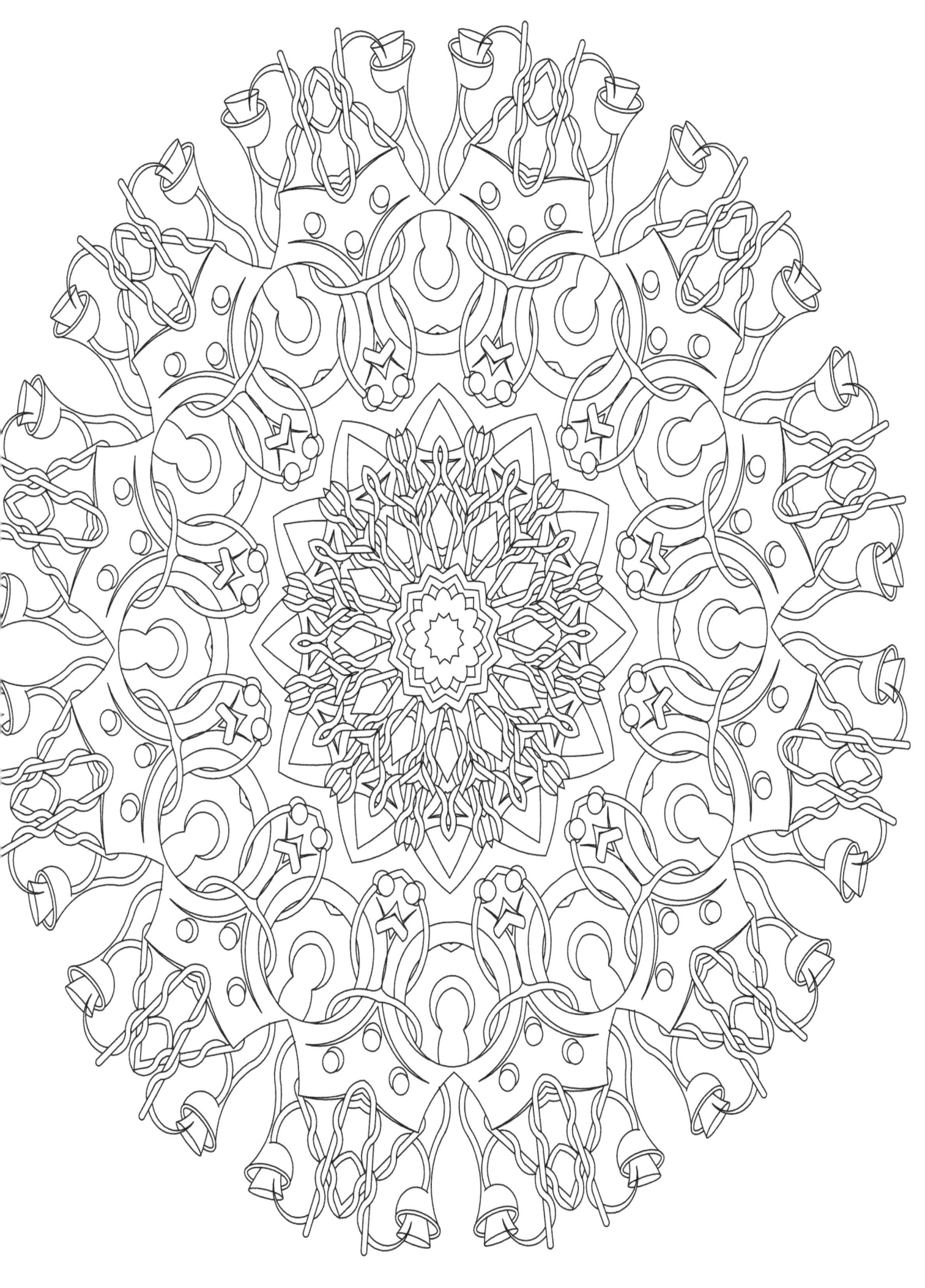

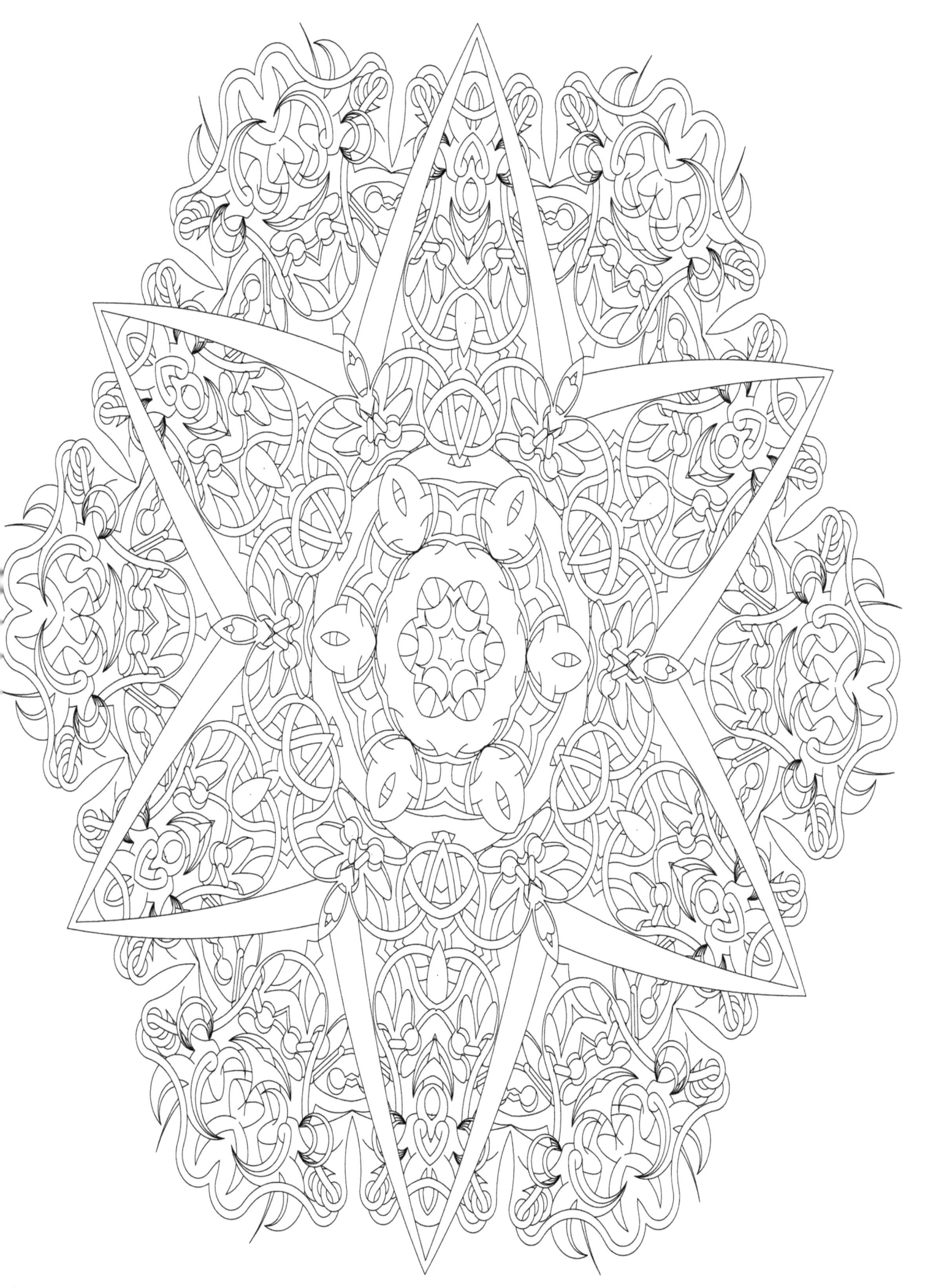

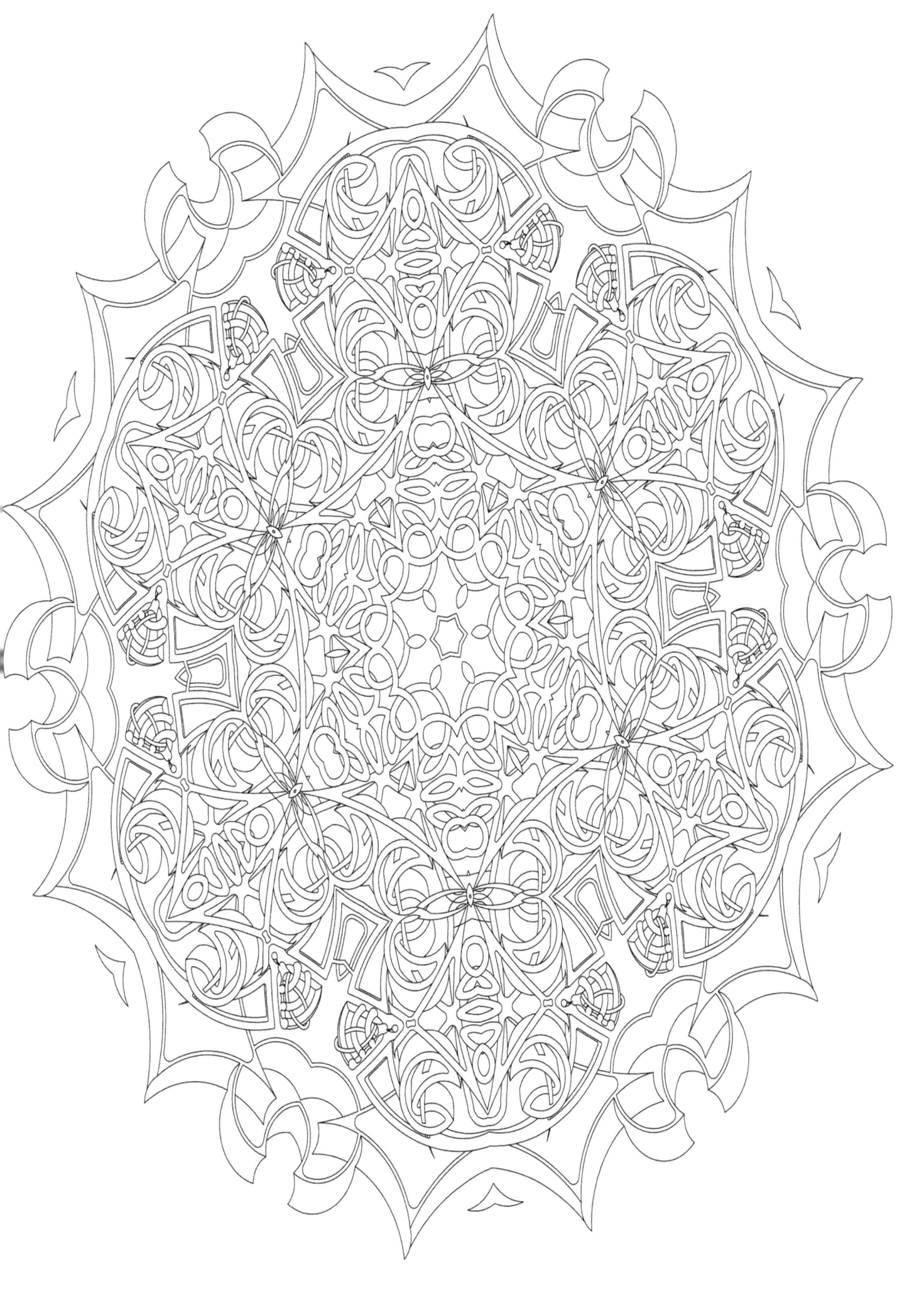

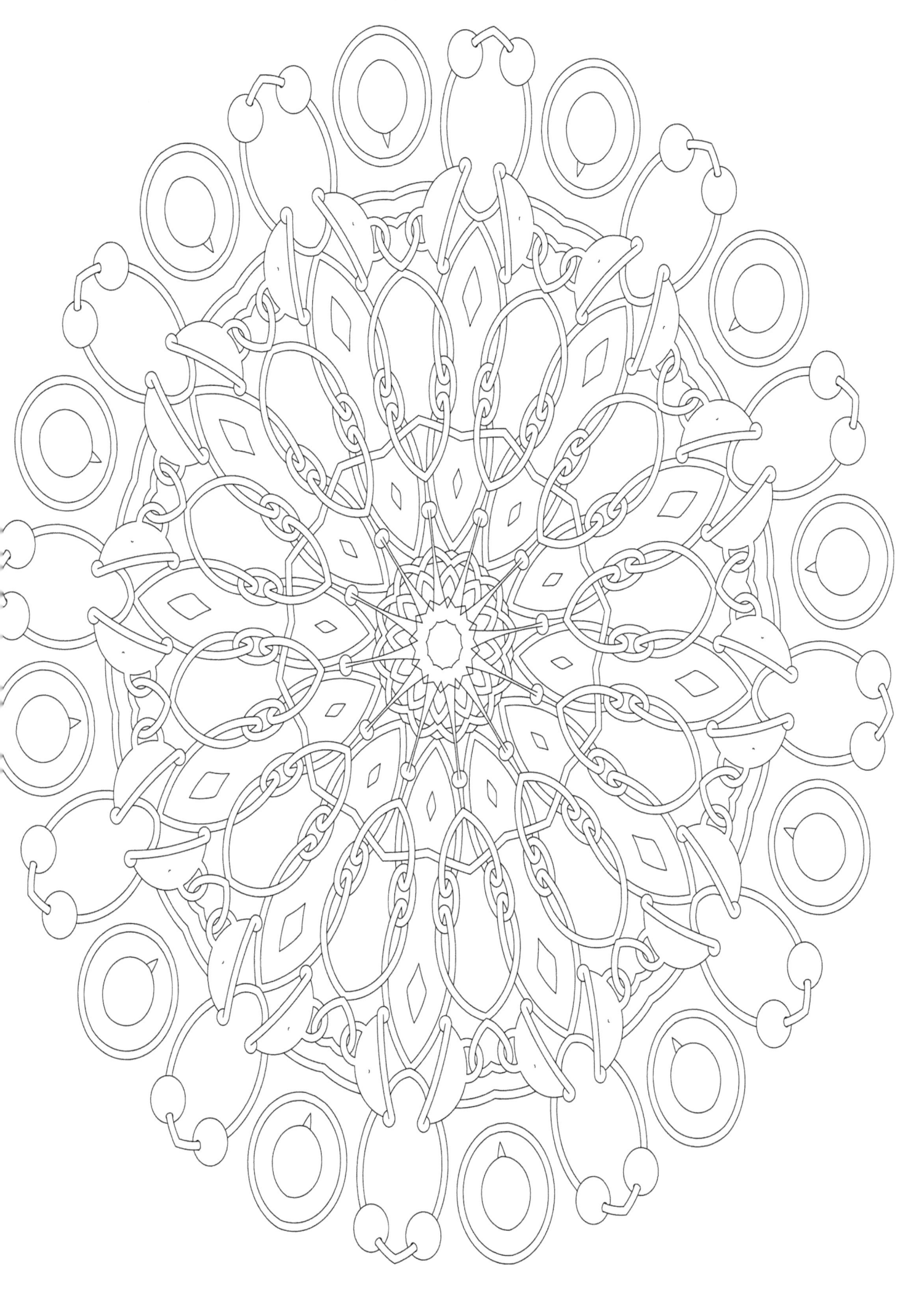

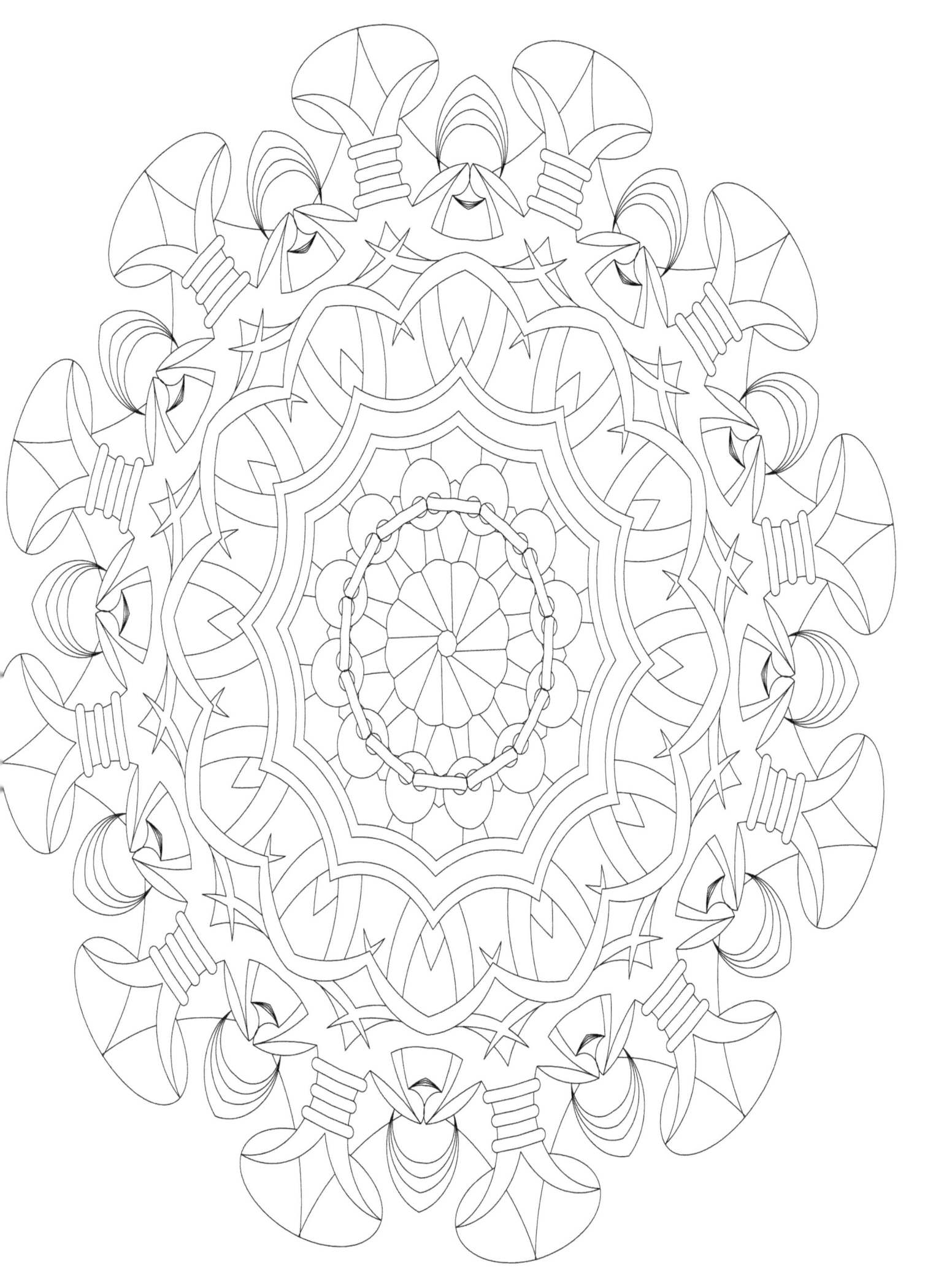

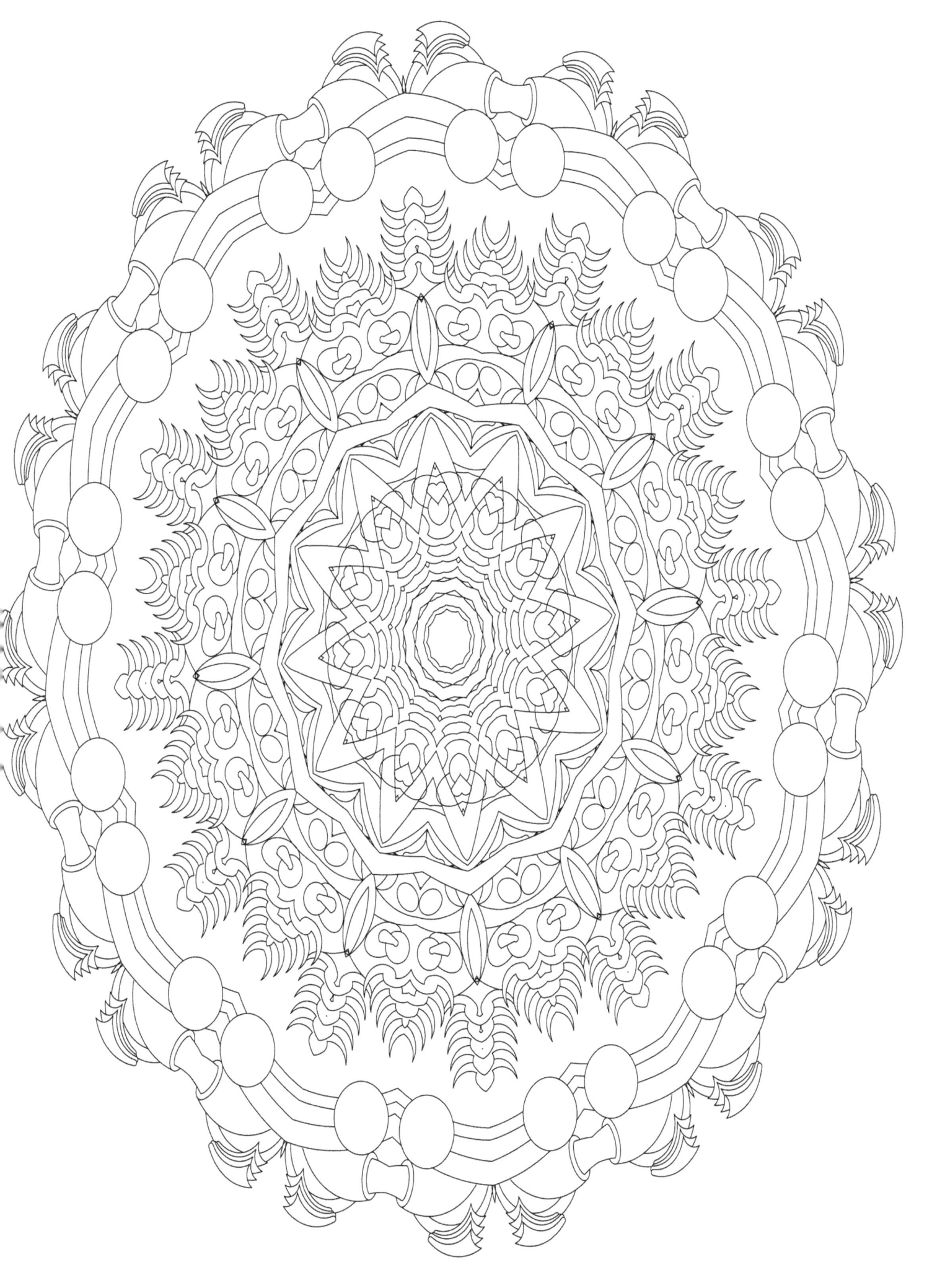

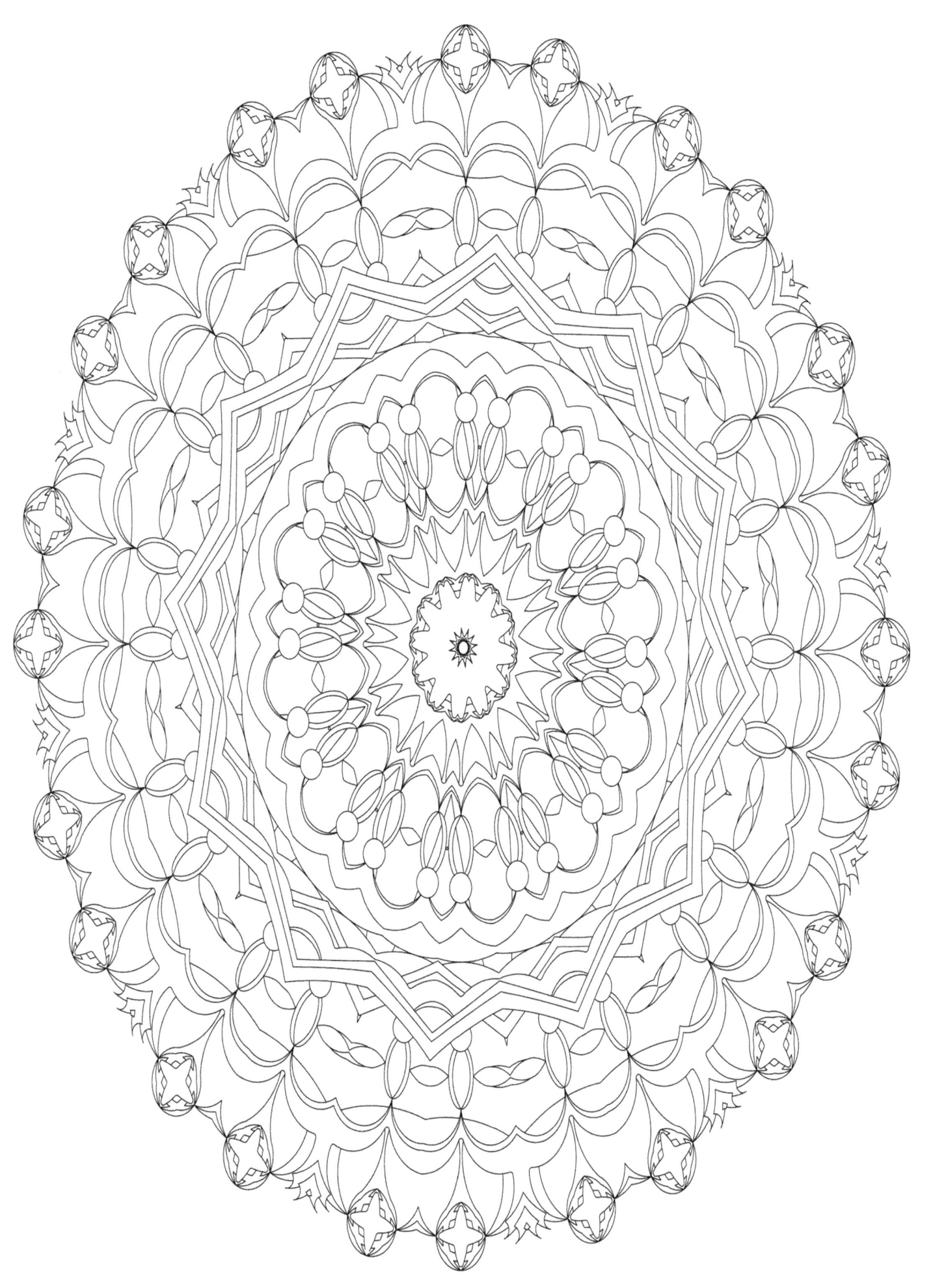

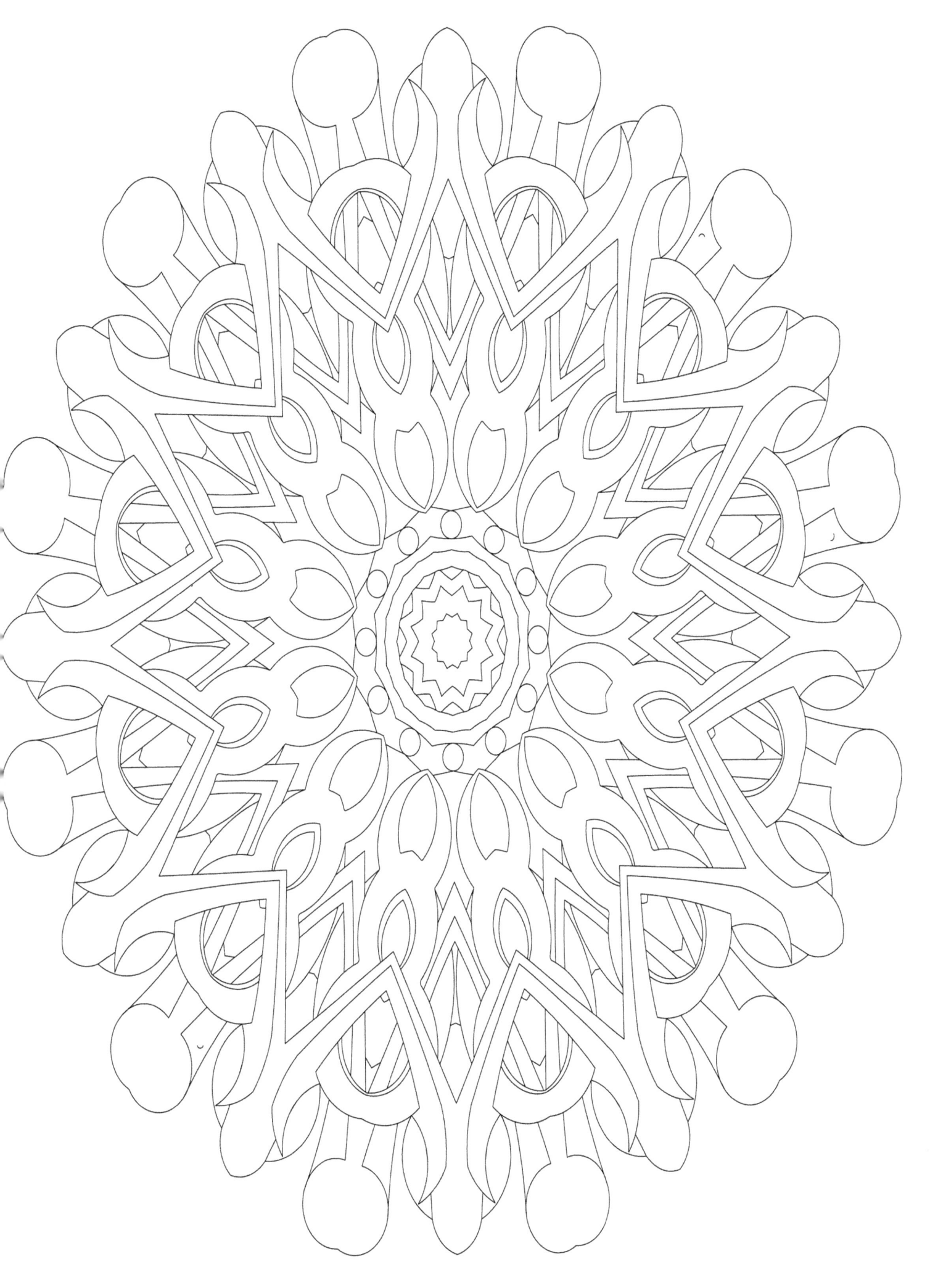

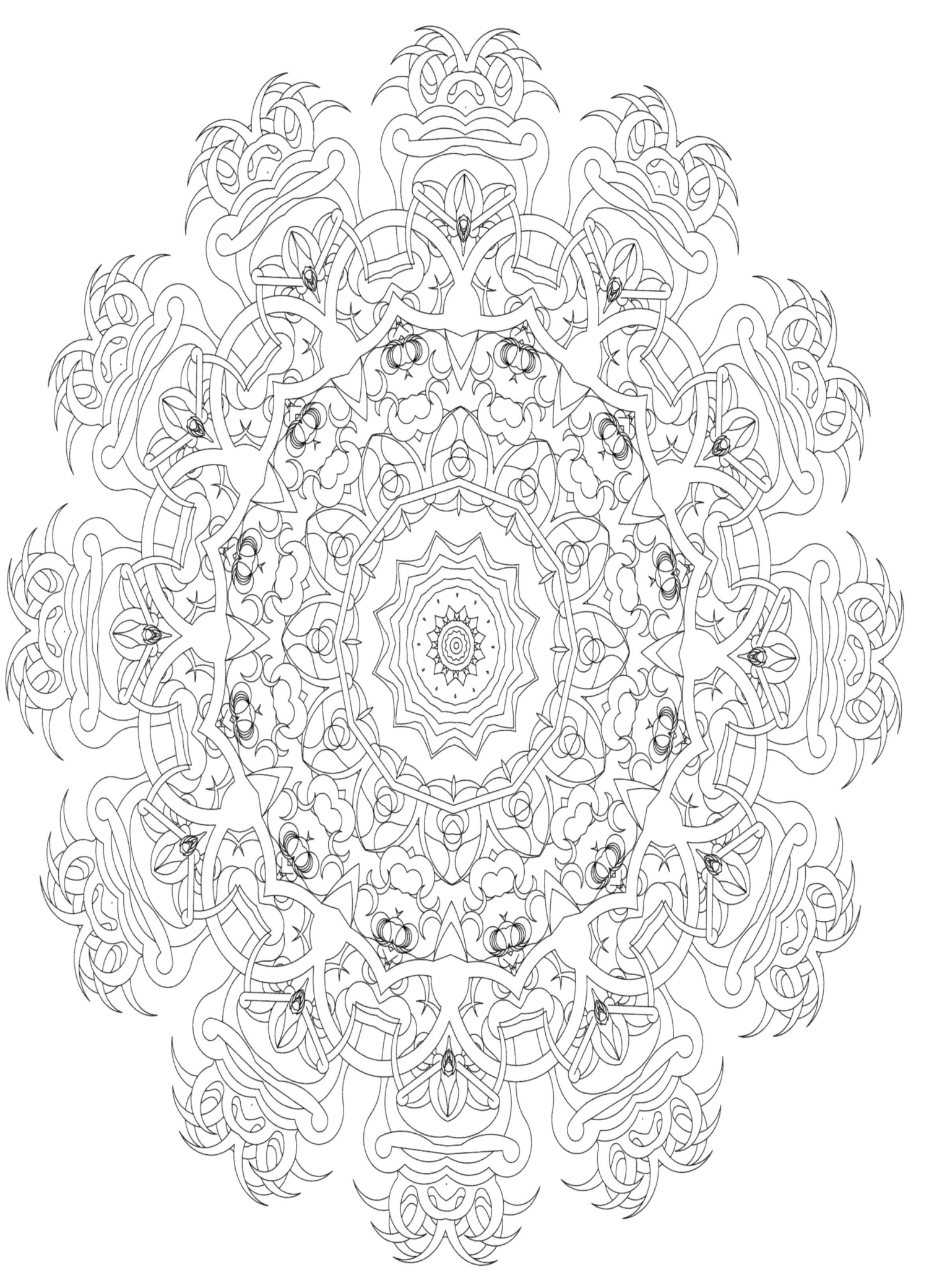

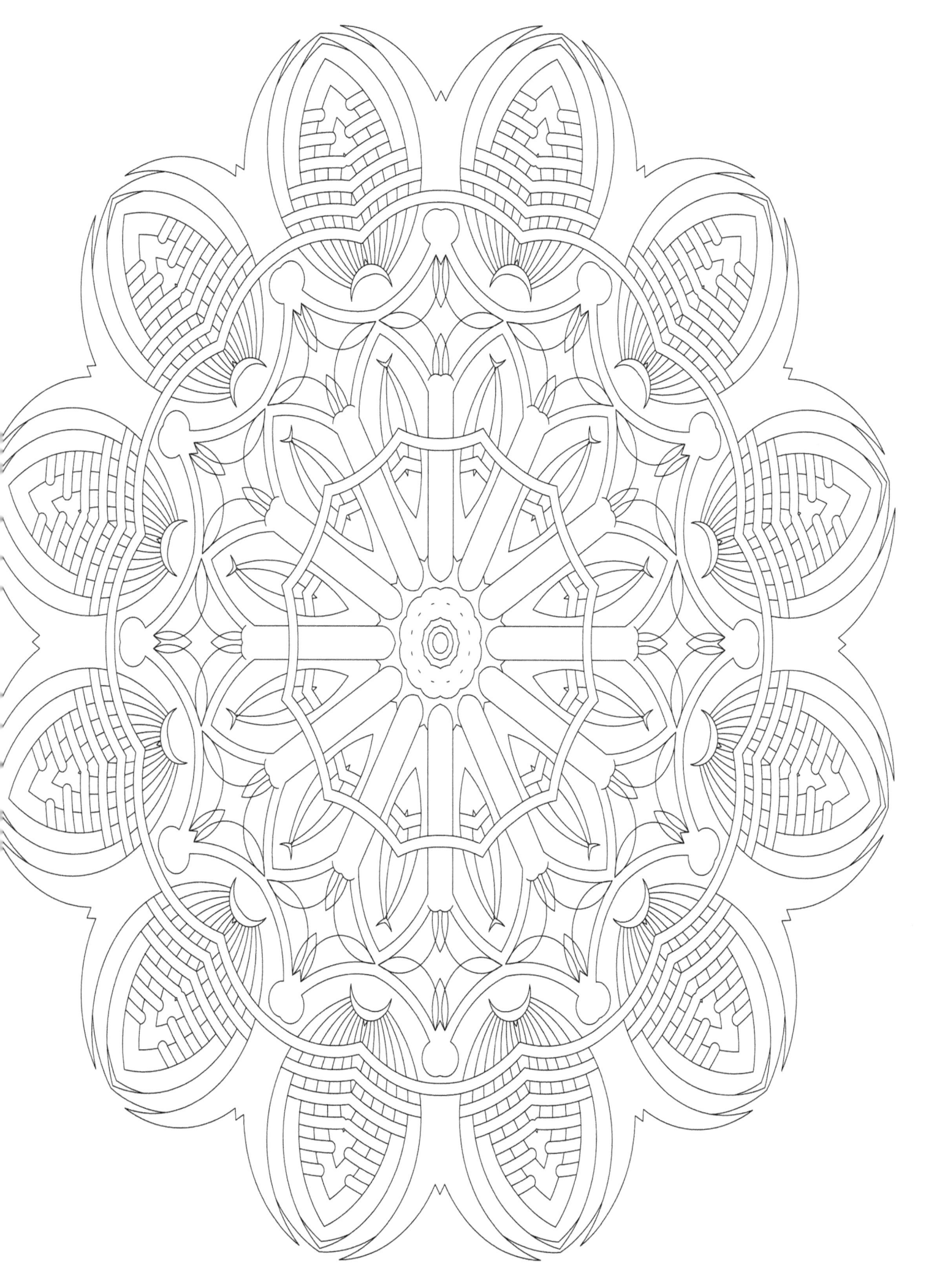

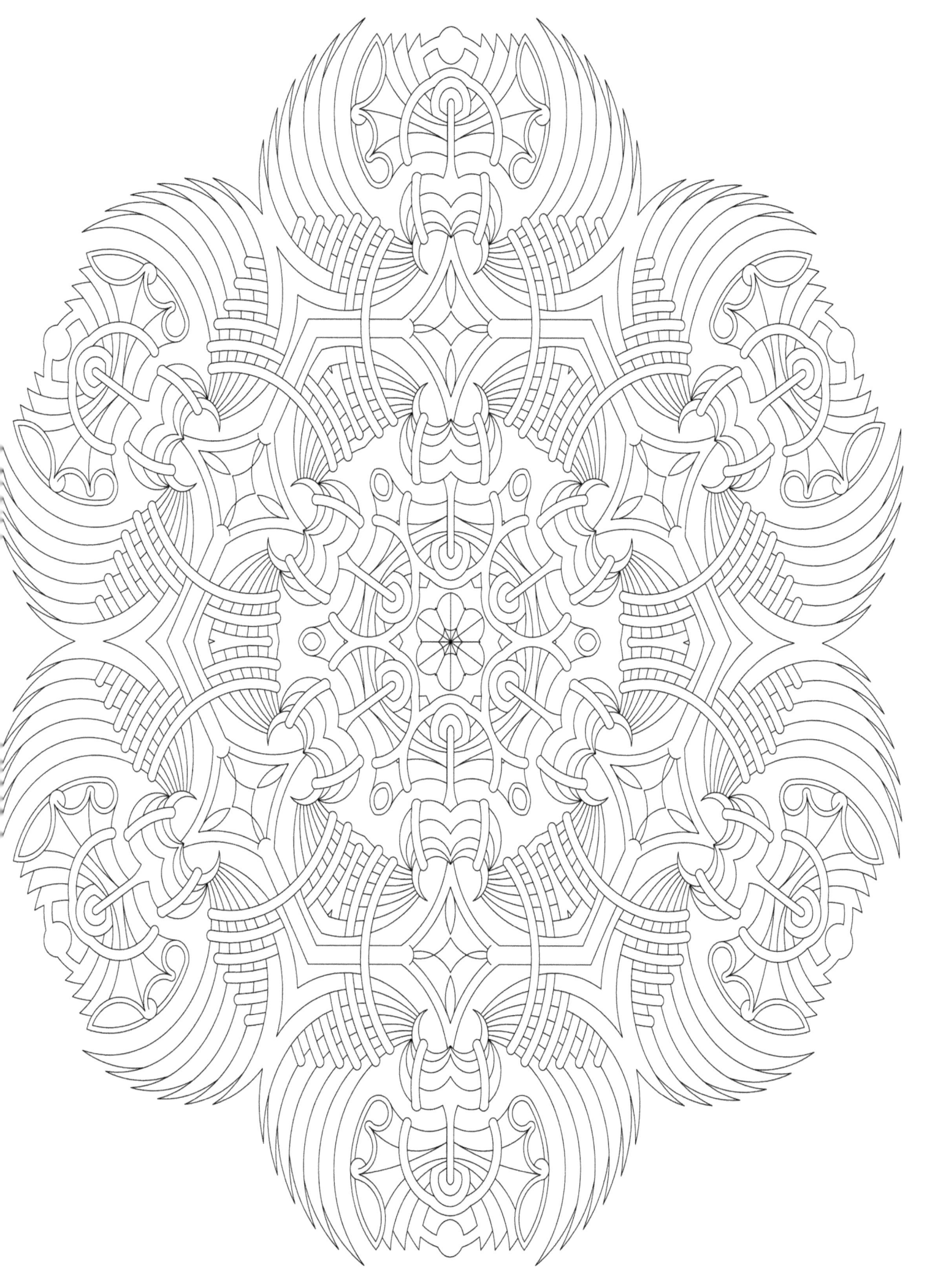

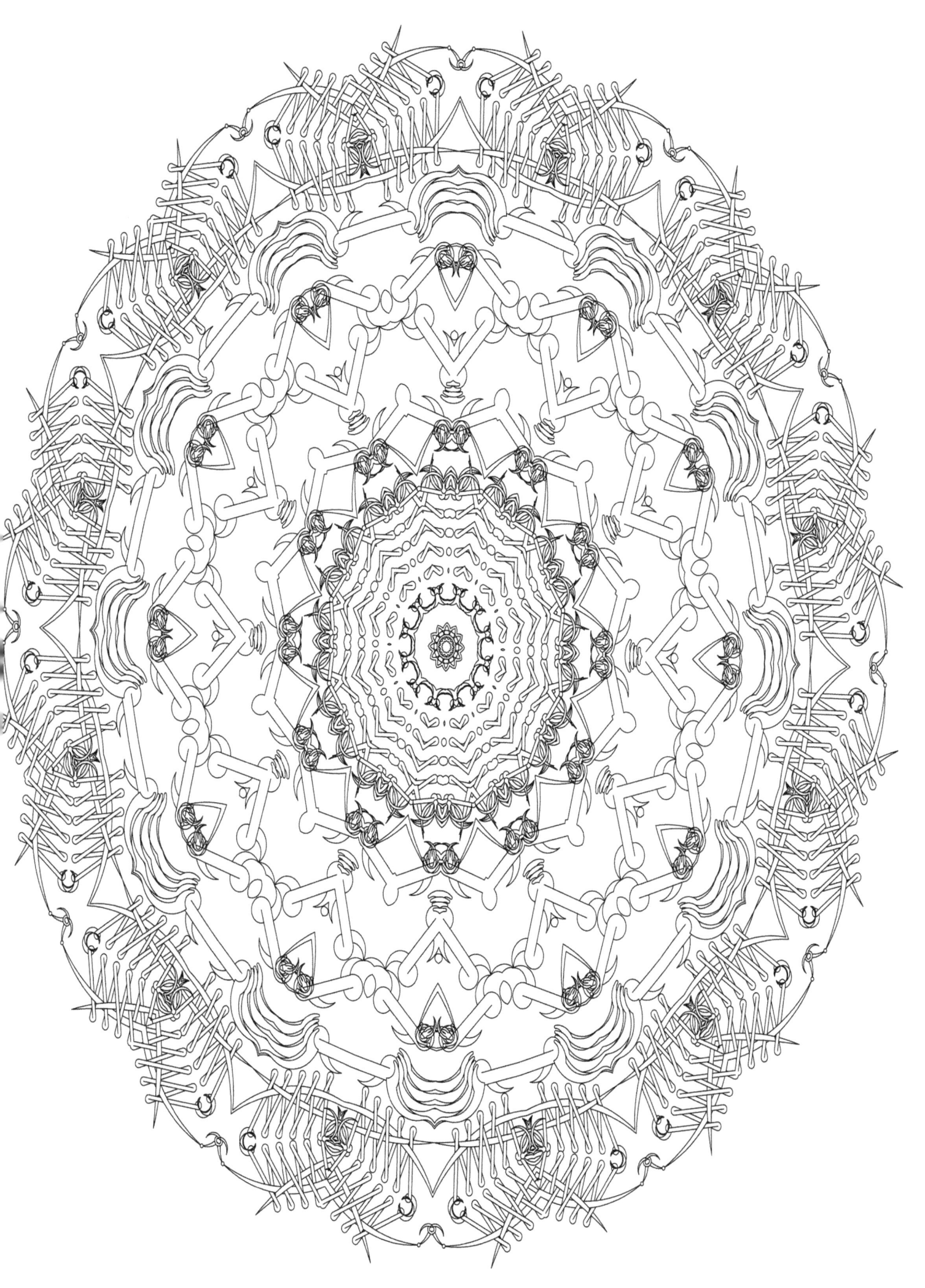

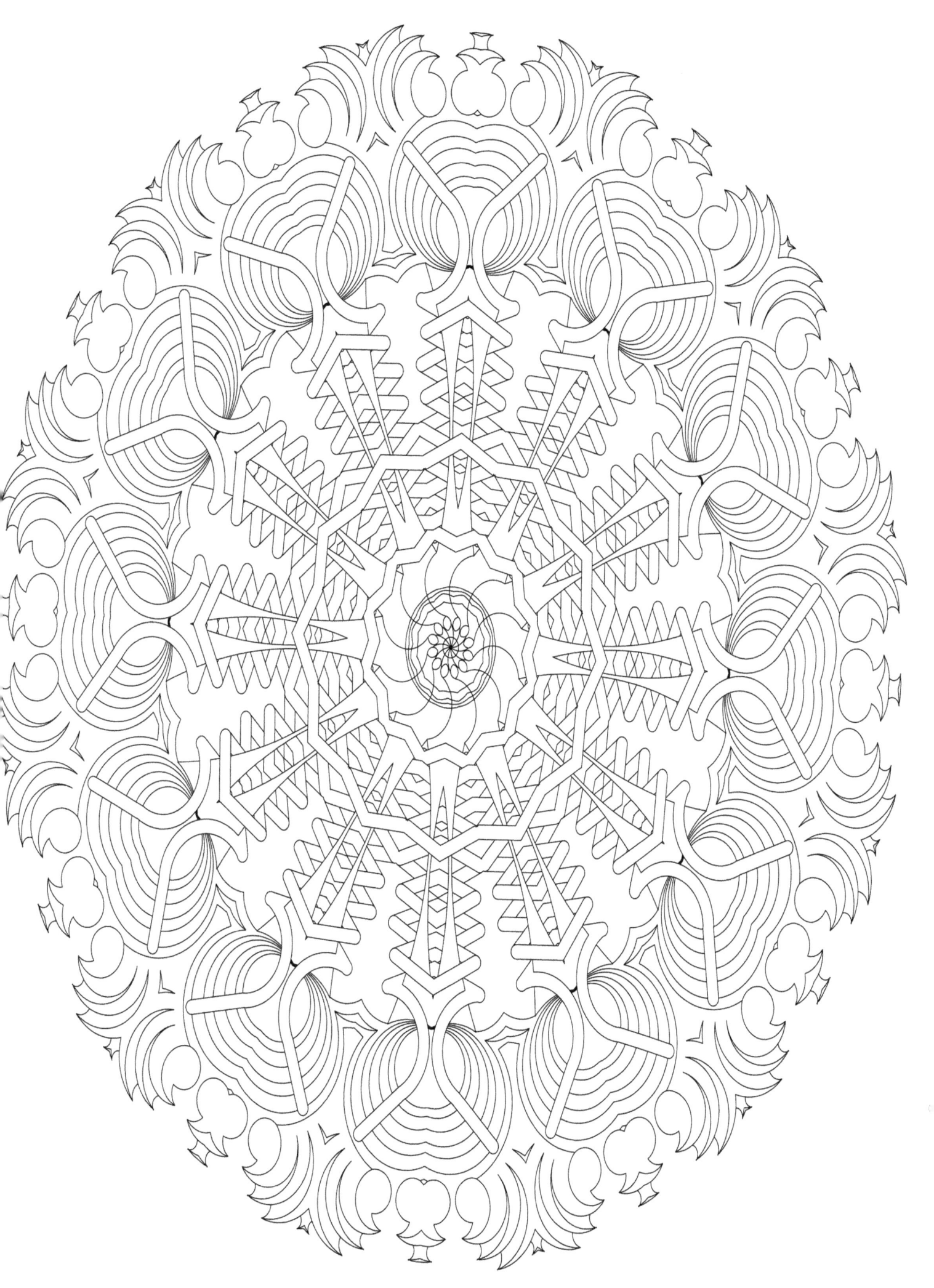

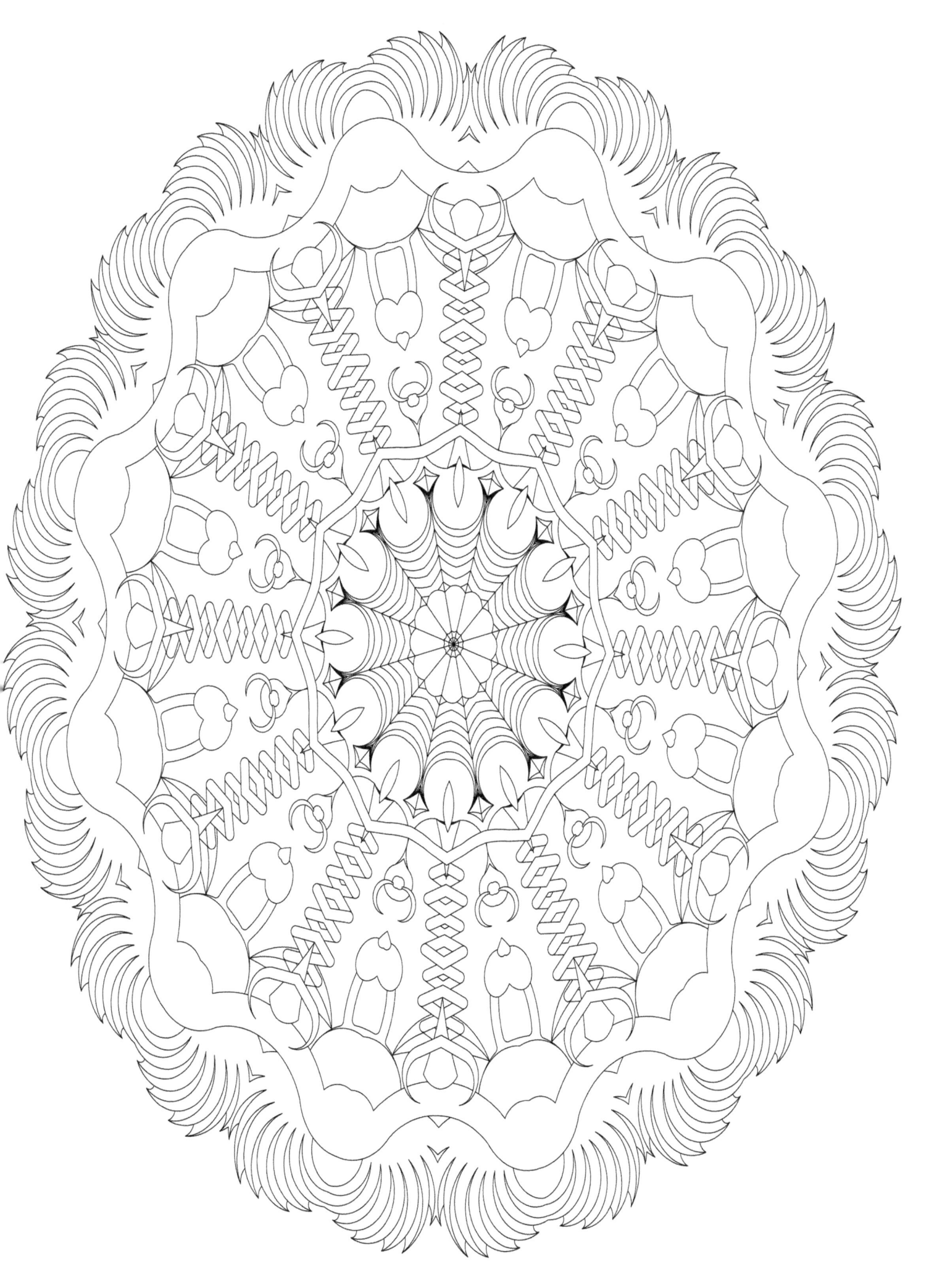

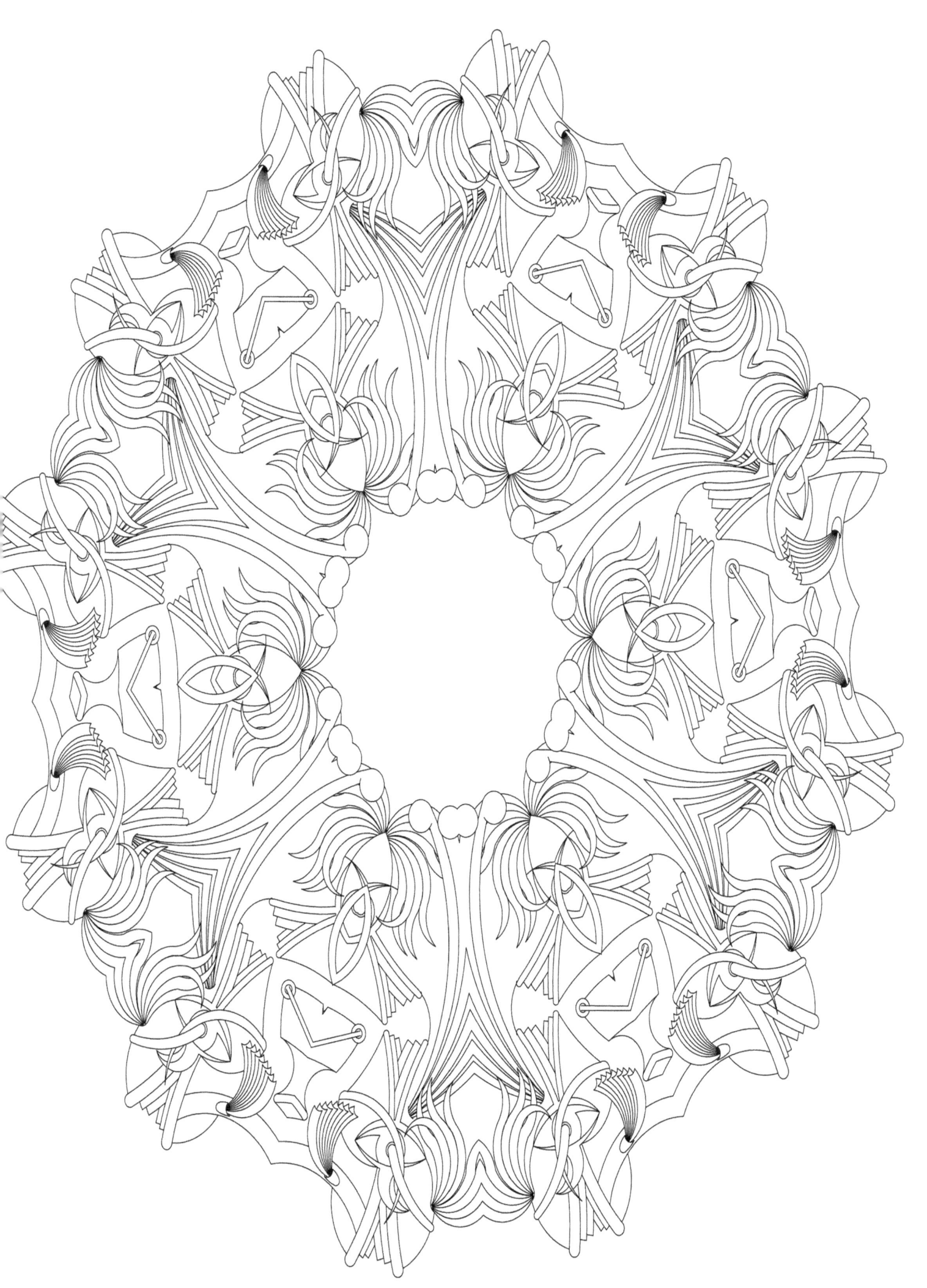

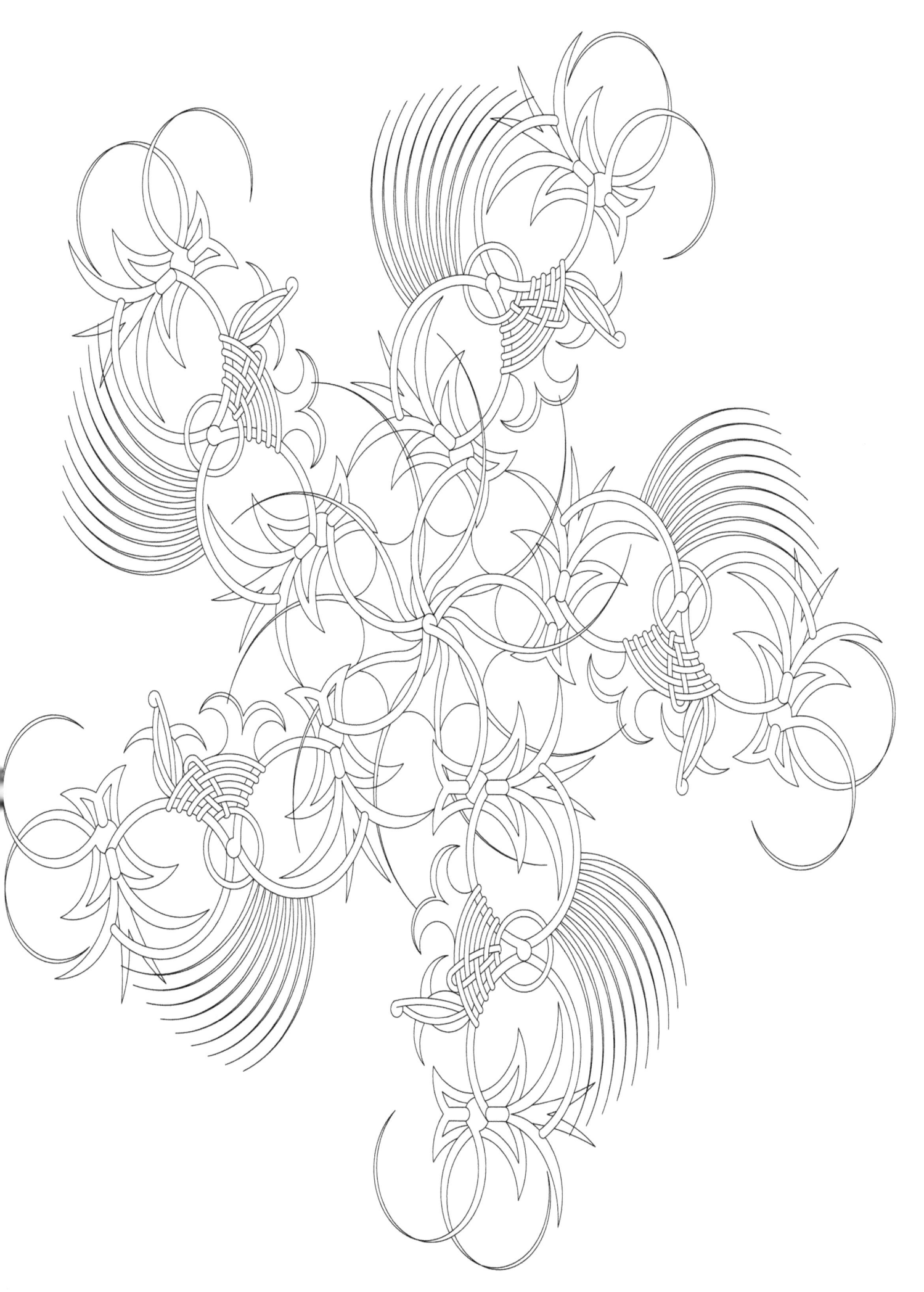

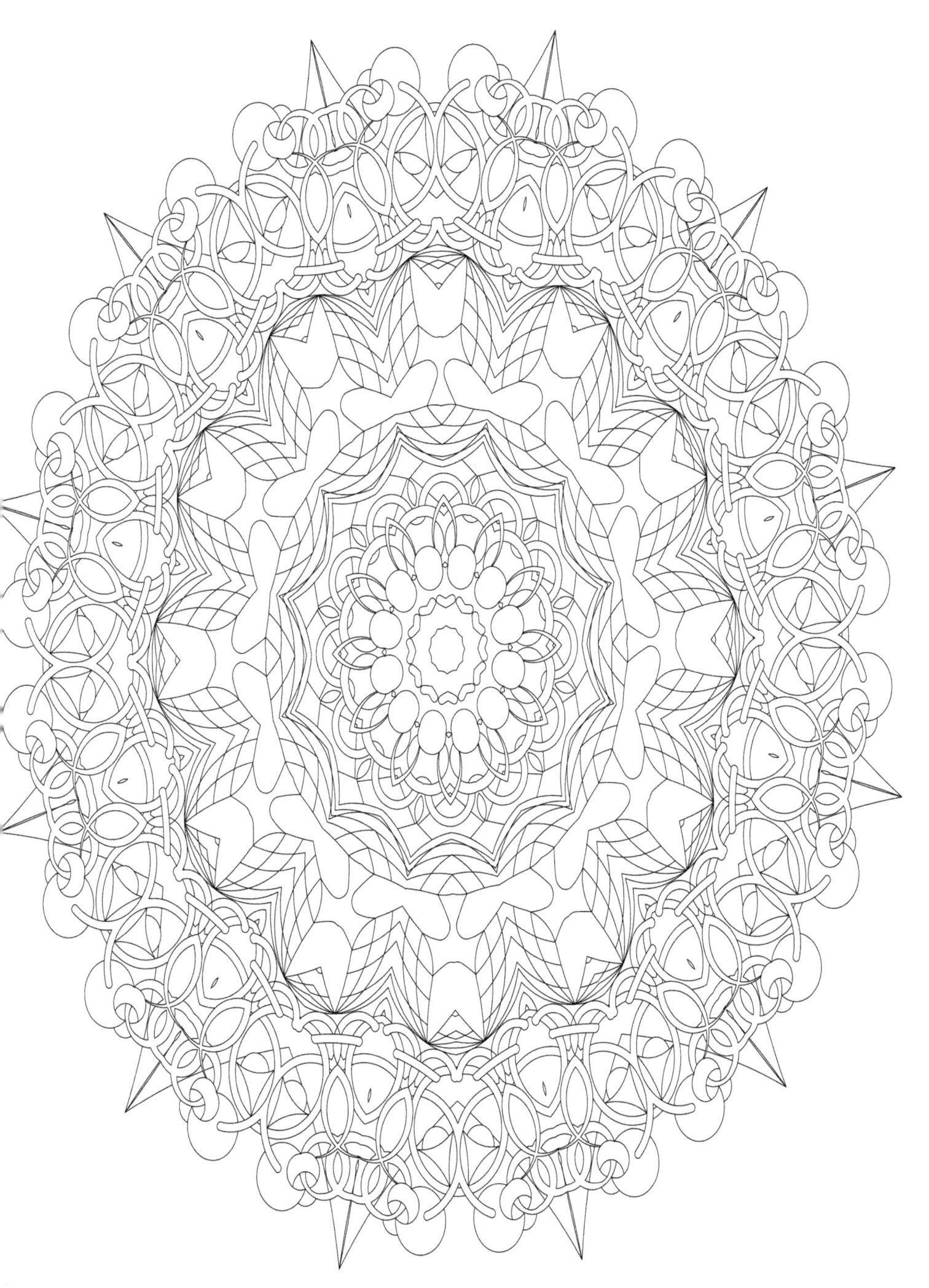

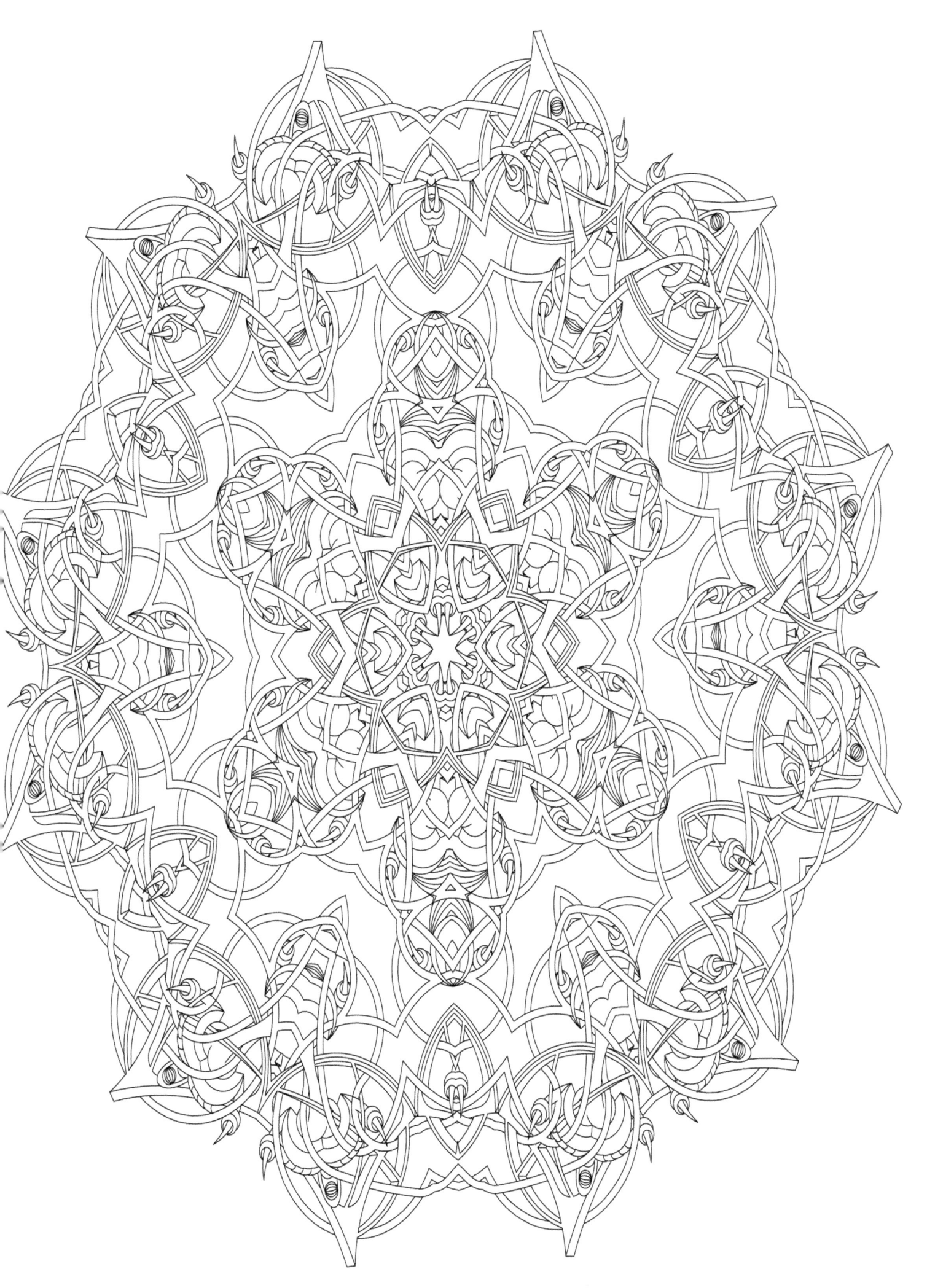

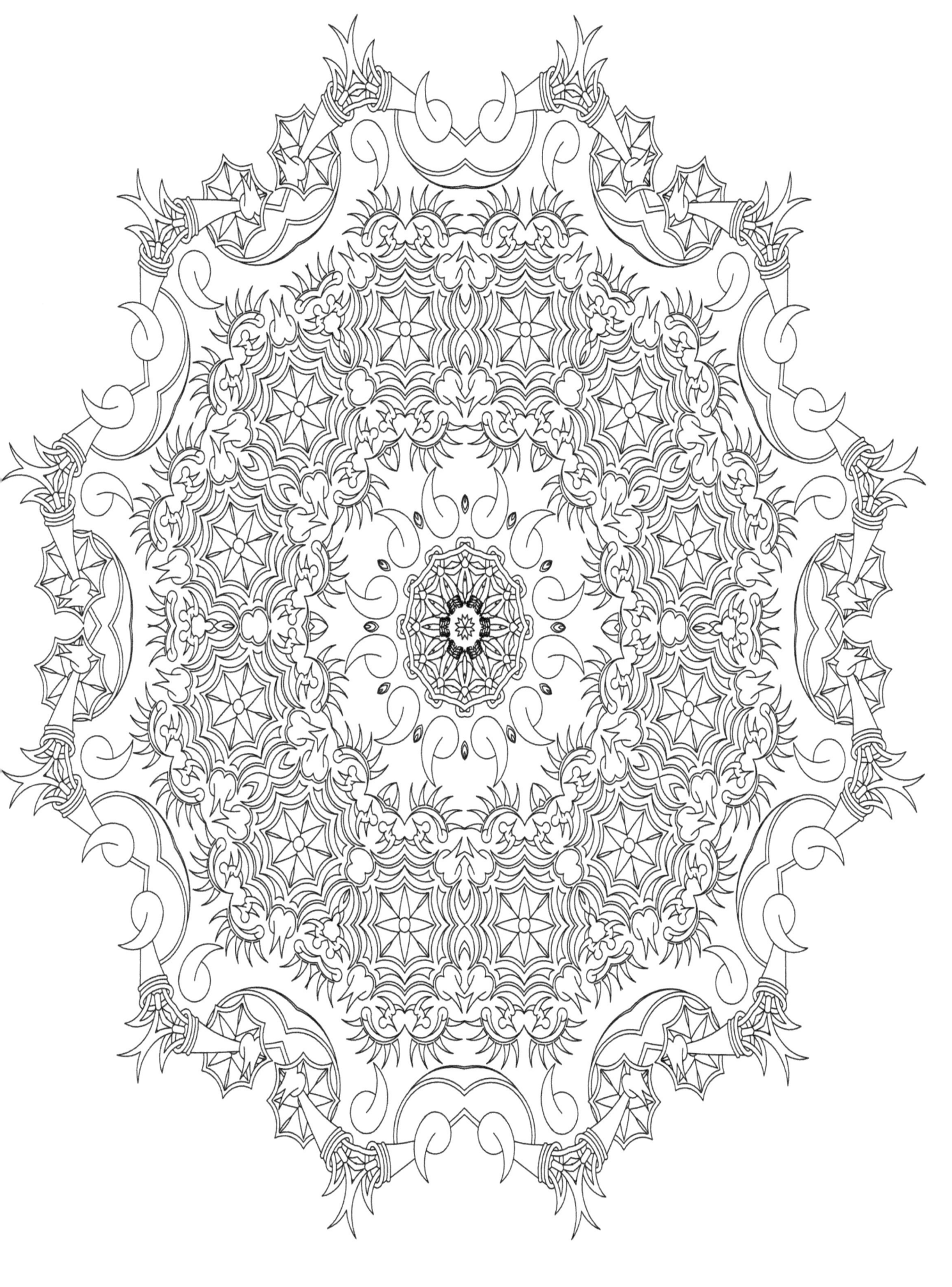

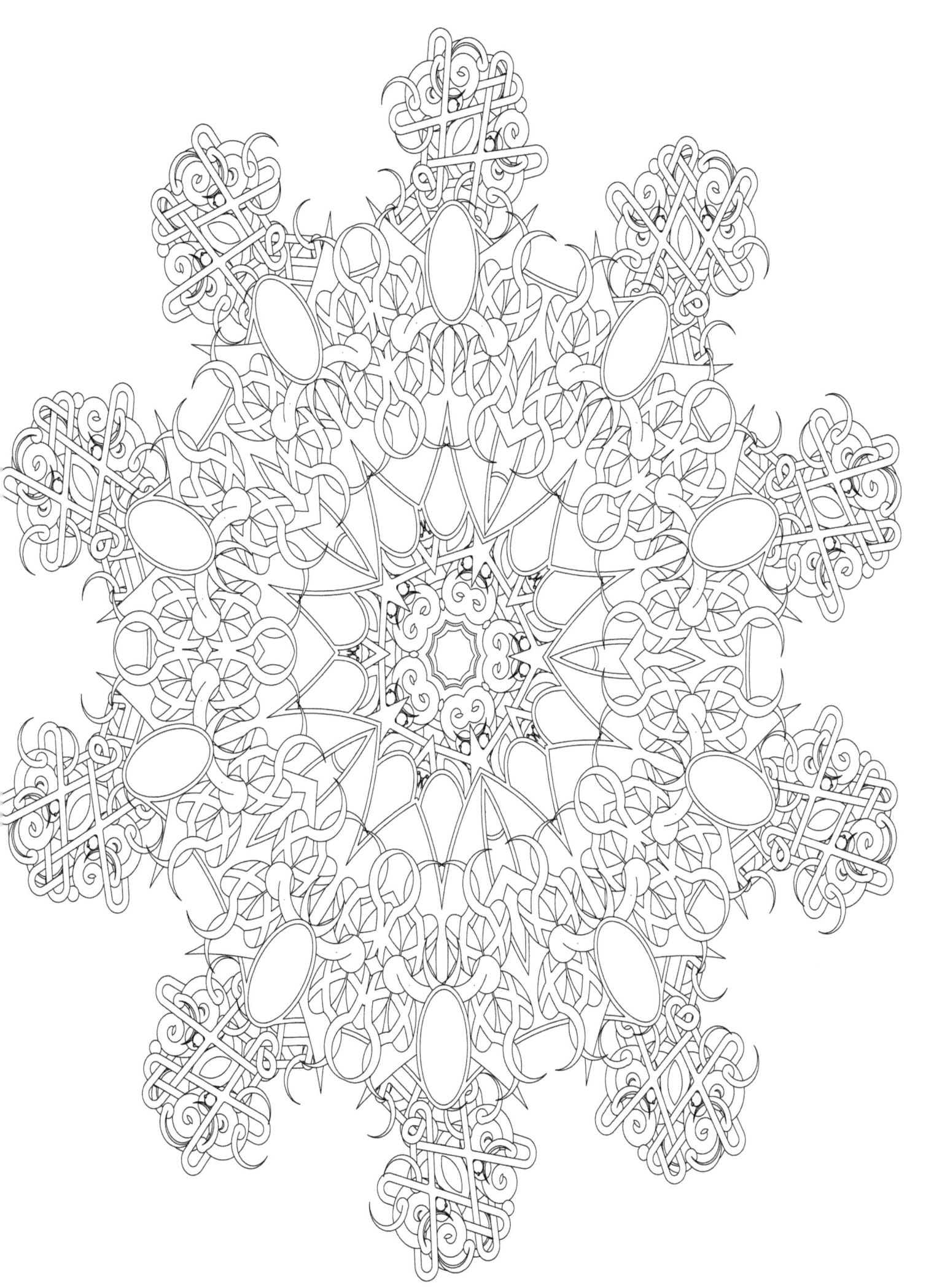

www.ingramcontent.com/pod-product-compliance
Lightning Source LLC
Chambersburg PA
CBHW081727220526

45468CB00008B/2009